Dear Paul,

May you continue
to hit it long & straight.

Regards
Mitchell
Spearman.

A·I·M

OF
GOLF

VISUAL-IMAGERY LESSONS
TO IMPROVE EVERY ASPECT
OF YOUR GAME

MITCHELL SPEARMAN
WITH HARRY HURT III
FOREWORD BY DEEPAK CHOPRA

RODALE

Printed in the United States of America
Rodale Inc. makes every effort to use acid-free ∞, recycled paper ♻ .

Quotes from Robin S. Vealey and Susan M. Walter on pages 6, 7, and 15 are reprinted from *Applied Sports Psychology*, edited by Jean M. Williams (Mayfield, 1992), with the permission of The McGraw-Hill Companies.

Book design by Swell Design

Library of Congress Cataloging-in-Publication Data

Spearman, Mitchell.
    A.I.M. of golf : visual-imagery lessons to improve every aspect of your game /
by Mitchell Spearman with Harry Hurt III ; foreword by Deepak Chopra.
       p.   cm.
    Includes index.
    ISBN 1–57954–805–9 hardcover
    1. Golf—Study and teaching.   2. Imagery (Psychology)   I. Title: AIM of golf.
II. Hurt, Harry.   III. Title.
GV962.5.S64   2004
796.352'3—dc22   2004001258

Distributed to the book trade by St. Martin's Press

2 4 6 8 10 9 7 5 3 1 hardcover

RODALE

WE **INSPIRE** AND **ENABLE** PEOPLE TO IMPROVE
THEIR LIVES AND THE WORLD AROUND THEM

FOR MORE OF OUR PRODUCTS
WWW.RODALESTORE.COM
(800) 848-4735

In loving memory of my father,
and to my mother and sister.

Contents

Foreword

I met Mitchell Spearman a few years ago, when I had just started playing golf. Being a student and teacher of spiritual principles and having applied these principles to my life over the years has allowed me to stay centered, grounded, and in present-moment awareness almost all of the time. This enviable state of consciousnesses came close to being shattered when I started playing golf! It was too frustrating, and for the first time in years, I started getting attached to results.

When Mitchell and I first spoke, he remarked, "The spiritual stuff you think about is something I frequently experience on the golf course. I wish I could experience it when I'm not playing golf!" I responded, "That's how I feel most of the time, but I lose it when I play golf." We made a deal. I would teach Mitchell the rules that make the game of life a joyful, ecstatic expression. Mitchell would teach me the rules that make the game of golf a joyful, ecstatic experience. Guess what? They are the same rules, as follows.

Mind-body integration
Effortlessness
Present-moment awareness
Learning from mistakes but not being victimized by them
Harnessing the power of intention
Being passionate and detached at the same time
Transcendence

Transcendence is the experience all spiritual seekers yearn for. If you've ever holed a 45-foot putt or had a hole in one or hit the sweet spot and watched the ball soar in a perfect arc and a perfect trajectory, then you know what transcendence is. As I started to practice Mitchell's A.I.M. technique, I began to realize that Mitchell was intuitively tapping into what the ancient wisdom traditions call the *subtle body* or what I have referred to in my books as the *quantum mechanical body*. Since ancient times, these techniques have been taught in various forms in sports such as archery, fencing, and martial arts such as aikido and judo. They are also part of the teaching of tai chi and various forms of yoga. They all have one principle in common: When you perfect something in your subtle body, the body of consciousness, it gets perfected in your physical body. Every aspect of golf—grip, alignment, posture, swing, putting, stance, chipping, bunker shots—must be first perfected in consciousness.

A.I.M. stands for actual vision, imagined vision, and mirror vision. Here, "vision" includes visual experience, auditory experience, and kinesthetic experience. Practice these techniques and you'll see your game soar—literally. Moreover, as you become more process oriented instead of being attached to results, your score will automatically improve. This is passion with detachment.

Mitchell Spearman is one of the most sought after golf coaches in the world, having coached golf professionals including Nick Faldo, Greg Norman, and many other greats. The reason for his success is clear: He understands both mechanics and consciousness. And he knows that when something is mastered in consciousness, it become reality in the physical body and the physical world.

Read this book carefully and follow and practice its principles. It does not matter whether you are an amateur or a professional, you will increase your enjoyment of golf, your scores will improve dramatically, and you friends will admire you and want to know your secret. Share it with them.

Good luck, and par for the course.

—DEEPAK CHOPRA

Author of *Golf for Enlightenment: The Seven Lessons for the Game of Life*

Acknowledgments

First off, I must offer thanks to literary agent **Mark Reiter** for his vision
and persistence in helping me bring my visual-imagery instructional methods from
the lesson tee to the pages of this book.

To the most important person in my life, **Joanna Dove**, for her skills at organizing
and coordinating this project and every other aspect of our lives.

To my **Aunt Marley**, a wonderful golfer who has been a great inspiration to me.

To executive editor **Jeremy Katz** for understanding and believing in the vision for the book.

To my coauthor, **Harry Hurt III**, who is a fine golfer himself and who was
as excited to write the book as he was to apply its techniques.

Much gratitude to photographer **Glyn Howells**, who, as evidenced by the photo
on this page, brought a truly new and unique perspective to the way
golf instructional photos are seen.

To **Isleworth Golf and Country Club** for their support and for allowing me
to use their wonderful facilities for the book's outdoor shots.

To **Amy Reynolds** at Nike, for keeping me well-oufitted with both equipment and attire.

To *Golf Magazine*, who in 1999 first published an article highlighting
my visual-imagery techniques.

To my editor, **Kathryn C. LeSage**, for her attention to detail
in bringing together words and images.

To all my friends, whose support over the years has been invaluable to me.

Finally, I express my appreciation to all the students who have joined me
on the practice tee. Without them, I would not be the teacher that I am today—
in their willingness to improve, my knowledge grew.

Introduction

Arguably the greatest golfer of all time calls it "going to the movies," and he's been doing it since he was a young boy.

Every time Jack Nicklaus prepares to hit a golf ball, he watches a self-produced color movie in his mind's eye. First, he sees where he wants the ball to end up on the fairway or green. Next, he sees the flight path the ball must take to get there—the distance, trajectory, and shape of the shot. Then he sees himself making the type of swing required to hit the shot.

Finally, he hits the shot.

Sports psychologists have a fancy scientific term for the way Nicklaus uses visual imagery. They call it *visumotor behavioral rehearsal*, or VMBR.

I've come up with a simpler, more sport-specific phrase: A.I.M. to Play Your Best Golf.

Along with Nicklaus and most leading sports psychologists, I strongly believe in the power of visual imagery to enhance performance on the golf course. I also believe that visual imagery can enhance your ability to learn and improve your game and my ability to teach you the game, regardless of whether you're a tour pro, an average golfer, or a beginner.

But we've got to go to the movies together. I cordially invite you to not only read this book but also participate in it with me. Golf is a participatory sport. Improving your game with A.I.M. imagery is a participatory experience—if you really want to play your best golf.

A.I.M. is an acronym for the three types of imagery we'll use as learning and teaching aids in this book. *A* stands for the *actual* images you should see with your eyes as you look out at the club, the ball, and your own body from the perspective of your golf stance. *I* is for the *imaginary* cues you should see in your mind's eye—dynamic depictions of the key movements in your swing, incorporating both realistic and fanciful objects and actions. *M* is for the images you should see if you look in a *mirror* to check your positions.

We're going to A.I.M. these three types of imagery at every facet of your golf game, from the full swing to putting, the short game, and specialty shots. We'll learn how to use A.I.M. imagery on the lesson tee, the practice range, the putting green, the golf course, even in your own home or office. I think you'll quickly discover, as I have, that A.I.M. imagery is the fastest, most effective, and most enjoyable way of "seeing" yourself playing your best golf.

All of us have probably used a form of imagery to enhance our athletic performance at some point. World-class athletes in sports ranging from track and field to football, basketball, and high diving, and top-ranked tour pros such as Tiger Woods and Annika Sorenstam, use imagery as part of their regular performance routines—with well-documented success. The most common use of imagery in sports is re-creating the performance of chosen role models: taking a mental picture of the swing of a great golfer so we can try to copy or imitate it later.

We can use imagery to re-create our own past performances, both successful and unsuccessful. And we can use imagery to create new experiences and ideal athletic movements that we want to perform in the future.

I've been using visual imagery since I was a boy. One of my earliest memories is standing in front of the mirror in the hallway of my family's London home, watching myself trying to imitate the swings of the top players I'd seen on television, in magazines, and on my local golf course. The more I practiced in front of the mirror, the better I got. I had no idea why, of course. I was just relying on my intuition, my instincts, and my experience. At the time, I didn't know a whit about the science of visual imagery.

I did, however, have a fine role model to emulate close to home. My aunt Marley Spearman (pictured at left) was one of the most accomplished female golfers in Great Britain, the winner of numerous important amateur tournaments. She inspired me to turn pro at a young age, when I started competing against the likes of future major championship winners Seve Ballesteros and Ian Woosnam.

When I decided to focus on teaching golf, I was fortunate enough to meet David Leadbetter, one of the most famous and most respected instructors in the game. As David's chief lieutenant, I served as director of instruction for the David Leadbetter Golf Academy, traveling the globe to oversee the opening and operation of new teaching facilities. Working with David, I developed a keen appreciation for the effectiveness of visual teaching aids of every form and description, ranging from beach balls, baseball bats, and giant fans to contraptions that resembled cattle prods. I learned that the greatest skill a teacher can have is communication, and communication can be visual as well as verbal.

I've had the privilege of coaching many of the best players on the PGA Tour and the European PGA Tour, including Nick Faldo (pictured with me, at right, at the 1990 Australian Open), Greg Norman, Colin Montgomerie, Craig Parry, and Curtis Strange. I've taught numerous corporate clients and hundreds of private clients ranging from top amateur players to average golfers and rank novices. And *Golf Magazine* has honored me by naming me one of their Top 100 Teaching Pros.

I've also been fortunate to have Harry Hurt III as the coauthor of this book. Harry is an award-winning journalist and broadcaster, an accomplished player and teaching pro, and an avid student of the game who has written three nonfiction biographies, two golf instruction manuals, and an account of competing on the pro golf circuit. Harry graduated magna cum laude from Harvard College, where he gained a solid academic grounding in the fundamental concepts of sports psychology and the use of visual imagery.

I'll be the first to admit that I owe a huge debt to all the many talented teaching pros I've worked with or read about over the years, including the late Harvey Penick. Although I never met him, I must credit the inspiration for the title of this book partly to Harvey's famous axiom "Take dead aim." Likewise, I owe infinite praise and thanks to all the golfers, great and not so great, whom I've coached and taught in my

career to date. I've learned as much, if not more, from all of them as they have probably learned from me.

My A.I.M. in this book is to show you and tell you how to play your best golf with visual imagery accompanied by intentionally brief text descriptions and explanations. As I'll keep reminding you, we're going to the movies *together.* Your active participation is essential to our mutual goal of achieving your full potential as a golfer.

In a sense, I'm asking you to be your own swing coach. Being your own coach allows you to take responsibility for the swings you make and the shots you hit. It doesn't mean forgoing lessons with a qualified instructor. It means learning about your own individual swing from start to finish, from your set-up posture and grip to your complete follow-through. It means finding out what works and what doesn't work, your tendencies when things go awry and when they go well. It means finding out what it takes for you to perform well out on the golf course as well as on the lesson tee and the practice tee.

Being your own coach also means doing a bit of homework. To make fundamental and lasting improvements, you'll need to learn about your swing at home in front of a mirror. You'll need to see and recognize what a good setup looks like, what a good grip looks like, what a good position at the top of the backswing looks like, and so forth. You'll need to develop the patience and discipline to check and recheck yourself with your own eyes.

I believe you'll get the most out of this book if you use it as a reference tool and guide in combination with practice and personal lessons from an instructor such as myself. Over the years, I've read literally hundreds of golf instruction books by the greatest players and teachers in the game, and it's been my experience that you can't learn to play golf or improve your game solely by reading a book. It's just not possible to put on paper all the necessary intricate details, all the complex dynamic movements that comprise a golf swing. And there's no way you can easily integrate huge volumes of written material into your swing—especially when you consider that a golf swing lasts 2 seconds or less.

What's more, every golfer is a unique individual. A book can't know who you are—how old you are, how tall you are, how flexible you are, what kind of physique you have, whether you have any restrictive injuries. A book can't assess your current ability or your potential for improvement. It can't prescribe a cure for swing faults or a formula for success that fits every golfer. What works for you might not work for someone else, and vice versa. To be truly effective, golf instruction must be personalized—custom fit, if you will—to each individual student.

That said, I also believe that, regardless of who you are and what kind of golfer you are, you can still derive enormous benefit from this golf instruction book because of its unique approach. By emphasizing visual images and keeping verbal cues very short and very specific, I'll help you avoid one of the most common pitfalls that cripples both students and teachers: paralysis by overanalysis. I won't clog your mind with an avalanche of swing thoughts that prevent you from swinging freely when you're learning, practicing, or actually playing the game out on the golf course.

When I teach golf to my students, I always start by giving them a clear picture of where they are when they come to me and what they need to do to improve. I show them what I see as the strong points and the weak points in their golf swings. I can usually predict with great accuracy that the same tendencies will run through their short games and their putting strokes.

Once I have laid out an instruction scenario, I remind my students that they are ultimately responsible for their own improvement even though the direction is coming from me. For best results, this means awakening their awareness levels by showing them a video of their golf swing. I usually do that in my video room, where there are no distractions, rather than outside on the practice range, where they may be tempted to rush over and start hitting balls before they're ready.

That first video is often something of a shock. I can't tell you how many times a student has said, "Oh, I'm sure my next swing will look much better." Unfortunately, that's seldom the case. Slowly, my students begin to accept the fact that much more than a tip or two is required to turn their games around.

After I've thoroughly explained the causes and effects of their swing flaws, I personally demonstrate to my students what their swings look like. Then I demonstrate what I believe their swings should look like. At this point, it's their turn to start making the necessary changes. This process is done in stages and, in the early going, without a golf club in hand. I typically start with posture, showing them how to create a dynamic, properly aligned setup with the help of the mirrors on the walls of my video room.

With almost everyone, a major change in posture and setup feels strange at first, and understandably so. But my students are usually able to mitigate these uncomfortable feelings by looking in a mirror and seeing that their posture and setup look much better. To help the process along, I often ask them to review their old posture and setup on their initial videotape while glancing back and forth at their new posture and setup in the mirror. The stark contrast between old and new is unmistakable, and an acceptance of the changes begins to take hold.

As I go into further detail about key components of the swing such as the grip, the takeaway, the wrist cock, the downswing, and the follow-through, it becomes increasingly apparent to my students that thorough understanding and precision practice—not merely banging out thousands of balls on the range—are the keys to learning and owning an improved golf game.

Along the way, my students start to ask all sorts of questions. "Can I swing like this with my woods as well as with my irons?" "Is the ball position the same with every club?" "Can we go right out to the range and see if this works?"

My answer is almost always the same. "Let's get familiar with the changes one step at a time," I tell them. "Let's build from the ground up. Let's understand it, then do it, and then we can start to own it."

I like to build and reinforce confidence early on in a lesson, so I often shoot a second videotape of my students right there in my video room before we head back out to the range. I show them their more athletic posture, their better grip, their more smoothly sequenced backswing, and so on. That way, they don't simply have to take my word for it. They can see their new look for themselves. I've found this approach to have great success not only with my tour pro clients but also with club golfers, because it provides the building blocks to make fundamental improvements, not just quick-fix changes that don't last.

To get the best results out of this book, I recommend that you read it through from start to finish at least once before you focus on specific areas of your golf swing. It's a quick read, and you'll get an all-important overview of A.I.M. imagery, my teaching philosophy, and how various aspects of the game, from the full swing to the short game and putting, are related.

You'll learn how to make A.I.M. imagery come alive by activating the visually oriented right side of your brain as well as the analytically oriented left side. You won't be asked to call on your conscious mind to remember, much less attempt to master, 30 swing positions. The only swing thoughts you'll get are three and four word "triggers" designed to cue up corresponding dynamic images in your subconscious mind.

In chapter 1, we'll participate together in a series of imagery exercises designed to familiarize you with the general use of A.I.M. imagery by means of some specific examples. We'll learn how to apply the same basic imagery techniques to learning and improving the physical skills you need to play your best golf, and the psychological skills you need to avoid choking under pressure.

In chapter 2, we'll use A.I.M. imagery to master the fundamentals of the full swing. In chapter 3, we'll explore the basics of putting and the short game. In chapter 4, we'll practice specialty shots and the most effective drills you can use to correct any lingering faults and foibles.

At the end of the book, we'll take comprehensive "second" looks at the full swing through the unique lens of each type of image: actual, imaginary, and mirror. Where the preceding chapters present a selected mix of A.I.M. images to illustrate a step-by-step approach to the swing, each appendix focuses on overall coherence and continuity from a single-imagery perspective. These sections also offer you an opportunity to discover which type or types of images may be most suited to your preferred learning mode and which may be most effective in improving your own individual game.

You'll find you can rely on this book of A.I.M. imagery as a comprehensive primer on every facet of the game. You can also refer to it over and over again as a kind of golf swing repair guide for error-correction pointers when you practice. Or you can consult it right before you head out to the golf course, for ready reminders of how to fine-tune your swing.

You'll develop the ability to use A.I.M. imagery to make your own self-produced color movies, both on the practice range and out on the golf course, so that you can A.I.M. for success, whether you're playing for fun with your regular weekend foursome or competing in a high-stakes tournament.

Okay, then—let's get cracking!

A.I.M.
for SUCCESS

Hello. I'm Mitchell Spearman, and the photograph on the previous page shows me standing on the first tee of my home course at Isleworth Golf and Country Club in Windermere, Florida. Take a few moments to examine that photo and the ones on this and the following pages, focusing your attention on the scene, the setting, and all the details. The tee box. The flowers and trees to the left of the tee. The fairway, and the green beyond.

Does anything strike you as familiar? Maybe you've visited Isleworth, and you've already seen what the first tee looks like. Maybe the first tee at my home course looks a bit like the first tee at your own home course. Or maybe the photographs remind you of the first tee at another golf course you've played somewhere else.

Now that you've oriented yourself on the first tee at Isleworth, I'd like to invite you to step into the photograph and put yourself in my golf shoes. I want you to play a mental game of pretend—pretend that you are me.

From this page forward, I am your alter ego, your stand-in, if you will. Although I appear in all the photographs in this book, I want you to pretend that you are where I am, and that you are seeing everything I'm seeing. I want you to imagine everything I'm imagining. I want you to pretend that you look just like I look standing out there on the first tee at Isleworth.

You may already be starting to realize that there are two ways to play pretend with visual imagery in general and with A.I.M. imagery in particular. You can visualize images from an internal

"I'd like to invite you to step into the photograph and put yourself in my golf shoes."

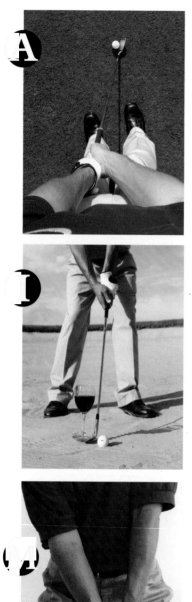

perspective, which means seeing things from inside your body through your own eyes. Or you can visualize images from an external perspective, which means seeing things from outside your body as if with the eyes of someone else who is watching you.

A.I.M. imagery enables you to see yourself and your golf swing both inside out and outside in, with *actual*, *imaginary*, and *mirror* images.

Actual images are seen from an internal perspective, as if looking with your own eyes. They allow you to observe the club, the ball, and the movements of your body from the vantage point of your golf stance.

Imaginary images are realistic or fanciful depictions of dynamic swing movements, incorporating familiar objects and actions. They're seen with your mind's eye, from either an internal or an external perspective.

Mirror images are seen from an external perspective, as if looking with eyes outside your body. They allow you to observe your stance and swing from the same vantage points that a teaching pro would.

Leading sports psychologists have found that most elite athletes visualize imagery from the inside-out perspective, and they emphasize the importance of non-elite athletes developing internal imagery skills. But they also agree that elite and non-elite athletes alike gain maximum benefit by utilizing both external and internal perspectives in their imagery. The key to success, they say, is to take the kind of systematic approach offered by A.I.M. imagery.

If you're among the millions of golfers who are unfamiliar with the use of visual imagery, at this point you're probably wondering what it is, how it works, and why it will help you play better golf. Let's find out.

IMAGERY IS REALITY

In the broadest sense, imagery is your mind's version of computer software. University of Miami sports psychologists Robin S. Vealey and Susan M. Walter define imagery as "a mental technique that programs the mind to respond as programmed." To the brain, imagery is the same as reality. Imagery does not require any physical props or outside stimulation. You can lie on a bed with your eyes closed, imagining that you are hitting a golf shot, and the experience will be just as real in your mind's eye as it would be if you were actually hitting the shot out on the golf course.

"Research indicates that when individuals engage in vivid imagery and absorb themselves into the context of their imagery, their brain interprets these images as identical to the actual external stimulus situation," Vealey and Walter report. "That is why imagery is so powerful."

Imagery is a "polysensory" experience, which means that it draws on input from all your senses. It's not just about seeing. It also encompasses hearing, smelling, tasting, and feeling. The more senses you can involve in your imagery, the more vivid your imagery will be. The more vivid your imagery, the more effective it will be in programming your desired responses.

The idea of using imagery to enhance sports performance isn't new, but its acceptance among the general public, golfers, and even the scientific community is relatively recent. The first modern research on imagery dates back to 1931, when experiments showed that imagining the bending of one's arm would create actual contractions in the flexor muscle of the arm. Jack Nicklaus personally pioneered the use of imagery in golf in the late 1950s and early '60s, calling it "going to the movies," but it wasn't until the late '70s and early '80s that sports psychologists began to conduct systematic studies on the use of imagery.

Over the past 30 years, the effectiveness of imagery in enhancing athletic performance has been confirmed by world-class athletes in a wide range of sports. In 1972, Colorado State University professor Dr. Richard Suinn demonstrated that downhill skiers could improve their times with the help of imagery. Soviet swimmers used imagery to improve their times in the 1984 Montreal Olympics.

Subsequent research has shown that imagery can enhance the performances of basketball players, gymnasts, field goal kickers, volleyball players, tennis players, dart throwers, and golfers. Various forms of performance-enhancing imagery are now used by over 90 percent of Olympic athletes, as well as by countless top players on the PGA and LPGA Tours, including Tiger Woods and Annika Sorenstam.

Exactly how imagery works remains something of a mystery, but there are four leading theoretical explanations. According to the "muscle memory" theory, vividly imagined actions produce muscular reactions similar to those produced by actual physical actions because the body remembers what the brain tells it. The "mental blueprint" theory claims that imagery helps code movements into symbols that make them more familiar and easier to reproduce, or blueprint. "Response set" theory holds that imagery is a stimulus-response proposition—that is, a particular visual image prompts a specific physical or mental/emotional response, just as the sound of a ringing bell prompted Pavlov's dog to salivate. "Mental set" theory maintains that imagery excites just the right level of arousal to focus attention on the relevant aspects of the athletic task at hand, a bit like "psyching up" for a big game.

Happily, you and I don't have to resolve the scientific debate over the way imagery works to make it work for us in improving your golf game. One of the few points on which all the theorists agree is that imagery is a cognitive approach, meaning it utilizes the brain and all the senses. As sports psychologists Arnold D. Le Unes and Jack R. Nation observe, "Cognitive approaches are most likely to be effective when the athletic skill has a large cognitive component." And few if any athletic skills have a larger cognitive component than golf.

EXERCISING YOUR "IMAGERY MUSCLE"

Before you can use A.I.M. imagery effectively, you need to get the hang of doing some basic imagery exercises. It's important to understand at the outset that the use of imagery is itself a skill that must be learned, trained, and practiced, just like a golf swing. Virtually all athletes and nonathletes possess the ability to use imagery. But as in every other area of life, some of us are better at it than others.

Learning, training, and practicing A.I.M. imagery isn't difficult, strenuous, or time-consuming. By definition, imagery can and should be imaginative, creative, and fun. But you do have to keep working at it on a regular basis. If you can devote a minimum of 10 minutes per day 4 days a week to imagery exercises, you should achieve noticeable results very quickly.

The first prerequisite is to get yourself into a calm, confident, alert mental state so you can relax and focus your full attention on the tasks at hand. Studies show that the more relaxed and attentive you can be, the more effective your imagery will be. Likewise, you must believe in yourself and have confidence that imagery can be effective for you in order for it to become a self-fulfilling process.

If possible, I'd like you to find a quiet, familiar place, maybe a private room at your golf club or a room in your own home, where there's just enough light to read this book. Hopefully, you can find a place that's comfortable and convenient, a place you can return to as our imagery exercises progress.

My own personal method of getting into a relaxed, attentive mental state combines meditation with a form of yoga. Contrary to popular misconception, you don't have to get down on the floor and cross your legs into the lotus position to meditate. I usually just sit in a comfortable chair. It doesn't matter what method you use so long as it works for you.

Okay, now that you're in a relaxed and attentive mental state, skip ahead for a few minutes and read through chapter 2 of this book. As you read, take time to study the mirror-image photographs in detail. Go ahead and pick up a club, stand in front of a mirror, and follow along step-by-step. Check yourself against the photographs. Compare the way your posture, grip, stance, and swing positions look with the way mine look. Try to make your look match my look. Do it all again with your eyes closed, feeling your way through. Then open your eyes and compare again.

Next, browse through the imaginary images. See which ones catch your eye and inspire your imagination. Try them out in your mind's eye, and with several rehearsal "swings," pretend that you are using—or,

even better, actually use—some of the familiar everyday objects that serve as props in the photographs. Along the way, you may think of new imaginary images of your own. If you do, that's great. Make note of the images that seem to be most vivid and appealing to you.

Finally, check your swing against the actual images you see from the perspective of your golf stance. Compare what you see with the photographs of what I see. Go through the same matching process you did with the mirror images. Adjust yourself and the club so that what you see matches what I see. By slowly rehearsing and re-rehearsing the desired looks and feels, you'll start to acquire the building blocks of a better golf game.

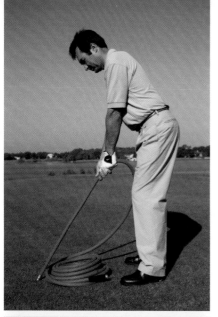

SEE THE POINT OF THE GARDEN HOSE

Now it's time to try using A.I.M. imagery to tackle a specific swing flaw.

Let's start by pretending that you're standing on the practice range at your own home course. Be as vivid and detailed with your imagery as possible. In your mind's eye, see the colors and contours of the grass, the shapes of the trees and bushes on the edges.

Use all your senses. Hear the chirping of the birds. Smell the leather of your golf glove. Feel the firmness of your grip as you hold a golf club. Taste the saltiness of the perspiration forming on the corners of your mouth.

Once you've fully situated yourself in the familiar environment of your practice range, let's suppose you've been struggling with your ball striking because you are somehow unable to get into the proper position at the top of your backswing. Maybe it's because you keep your arms too stiff. Maybe it's because you can't seem to swing the club on the proper path or the proper plane. Maybe it's because you're unclear about what the proper position at the top of your backswing is. The exact nature of your top of the backswing problem doesn't matter much. Just remain relaxed and attentive; we're going to get you on the right track in short order.

For the purpose of this exercise, we're going to start by using one of the imaginary A.I.M. images. Almost all of them illustrate familiar dynamic movements such as chopping wood, tossing a softball, or pointing a garden hose to spray water. Each image is accompanied by a verbal "trigger," a quick, easy to fire, and easy to remember catchphrase such as "Chop a tree," "Softball your pitch," or "Point the hose."

Speaking of which, I'm now going to ask you to see yourself assuming your stance and setting up just as you normally would to hit a golf ball, but instead of seeing yourself holding a golf club, I want you to see yourself holding a garden hose. The coils of the hose are lying on the ground in front of you, roughly where the golf ball would normally be. You're holding the nozzle end of the hose in your right hand with your normal right-handed golf grip.

Okay, without getting out of your setup, rotate your head to the left, and look out in the general direction of where your imaginary target line would be if you actually were going to hit a golf ball. Lo and behold, you see me standing a few feet away from you, just to the left of your target line. All of a sudden, you get an overpowering urge to spray me in the face with water.

Fair enough—I'm going to invite you to give me a thorough drenching. But you've got to spray me sideways from the top of your backswing. Just swing the nozzle end of the hose so that you wind up pointing it at me from a comfortably extended position to the right of and slightly behind the right side of your neck. Don't get sidetracked by pretending you're swinging a golf club. You're holding the nozzle of a garden hose. Just go ahead and point the hose.

Now spray me with water.

Nice shot; you hit me right between the eyes! In the process, you also reached a picture-perfect position at the top of your backswing.

If you don't believe me, let's introduce a mirror image to our exercise. Repeat your garden hose backswing in front of a mirror or a picture window so that you can check yourself out. Compare what you see in the mirror to the mirror-image photograph of my position at the top of the backswing, at right.

As a cross-check, let's use an actual image. Point the hose one more time. Note what you see from the perspective of your golf stance when you reach the top of your garden hose backswing. Compare what you see to the previous page's photo of what I see at the top of my backswing: your left shoulder behind the ball, blocking your view of your right foot.

There's nothing to it, is there? Nor should there be. Chances are you've sprayed your garden and/or someone standing in your garden many times in the past. You can easily handle a garden hose even if I ask you to point it at me sideways from behind your neck.

So see yourself doing it again several more times. Get a good sense of what you see, hear, smell, taste, and feel as you move the nozzle into the proper position to spray water in my face.

If we put a golf club in your hand, you can consistently reach the proper position at the top of your backswing using the same A.I.M. images and the trigger "Point the hose."

Come on—let's see it and do it.

Practice Movies

I want you to actually go out to your practice range with your A.I.M. imagery fresh in your mind's eye. You're welcome to carry along a real garden hose if you like, but in this practice range phase of our exercise, you're going to be handling a real golf club.

Start by gripping the club and assuming your stance as you normally would, and say your trigger out loud or silently to yourself: "Point the hose." Now, in slow motion, swing the club to the top of your backswing, re-creating the same sensations you experienced when you were spraying me with the imaginary garden hose.

Make 10 more slow-motion backswings, continuing to focus on what you see, hear, taste, and feel as part of your A.I. M. imagery. Then make 10 full-length practice swings from backswing to follow-through with your normal rhythm and tempo. Don't abandon your imagery by recalling any extraneous swing thoughts or tips you may have gotten in the past. The only verbal cue that should be running through your brain is your trigger: "Point the hose."

Reinforce your imaginary A.I.M. image with the corresponding mirror and actual images. Make a practice swing in front of a mirror with your "Point the hose" verbal trigger, and check yourself out. How does your position compare to the mirror-image photograph of me?

Make another practice swing with your "Point the hose" verbal trigger, and note what you see through your own eyes from the perspective of your stance. How does it compare with the actual-image photograph of what I see?

Once you've completed your practice swings, tee up a real golf ball and pick a real target out on the range. First, visualize the image of the ball nestled on top of your target. Second, visualize the flight path of the ball—the distance, trajectory, and line it needs to follow to reach your target. Third, visualize the swing you need to make to produce that ball flight. Fourth, assume your stance and set up, repeating your trigger: "Point the hose; point the hose."

Now hit the shot.

I can't guarantee that you'll make a perfect swing and hit a perfect shot every time. No one can. Indeed, I warn you to be wary of any teaching pro who offers an unconditional guarantee of perfection. There's no such thing. As Dr. Bob Rotella, one of the sports psychologists most respected by tour pros and top amateur players, points out, golf is not a game of perfect.

But I can assure you that if you learn, practice, and use the A.I.M. imagery in the chapters ahead as we've just done in our exercises with the garden hose, you will see yourself playing your best golf—the best golf you can ever imagine.

So let's put A.I.M. imagery to the acid test. Go ahead—try the garden hose image out on the golf course, and see how you do.

SEE YOURSELF WINNING A PGA TOURNAMENT

Okay, you're back from the course.

How did it go? I'm willing to bet that you made better swings and hit better shots than you did the last time out. I'll also bet you finished with a better score.

If you did, that's great. You've already experienced some of the effectiveness A.I.M. imagery can have in improving your golf game. But if you happened to play just as poorly or even worse than you did the last time out, don't despair. And don't give up on A.I.M. imagery just yet.

Remember, using A.I.M. imagery takes practice, just like your golf swing does. As sports psychologists are quick to remind us, the preponderance of evidence shows that the use of imagery can enhance athletic performance for most people. Even so, using imagery does not *guarantee* peak performance for everybody at all times and under all circumstances.

No imagery, A.I.M. imagery included, can take the place of physical practice at golf or any other sport. The experts I've consulted say that we should regard imagery as a kind of mental "vitamin supplement" to be used in combination with physical practice. "Imagery is valuable not as a *replacement* for physical practice," note University of Miami sports psychologists Vealey and Walter, "but as a way to train the mind *in conjunction* with the physical training of the body."

The best way to improve the effectiveness of A.I.M. imagery on your golf game is to strengthen your "imagery muscle" by using it as often as you can. You can use it in your learning and practice sessions, as I do. You can use it out on the golf course,

as Nicklaus, Woods, and scores of other top players do. You can use it as a tool for postround analysis. And you can use it as a tool to preview a round you're going to play at your home course or any other course.

I use one of my favorite A.I.M. imagery exercises in coaching tour pros to play their best and avoid choking under pressure. Along with pre-rehearsing strategy and shot making, we preview the environmental and emotional conditions they're likely to en-counter when they arrive at an important tournament.

I begin by asking my tour pro clients to see themselves at the golf course where the tournament is being played, to see them-selves walking among the spectators, the rules officials, and their fellow competitors. I instruct them to picture themselves teeing off in front of the large gallery. Eventually, I ask them to see their names at the top of the leaderboard in the final round. At that point, some of them remain cool and calm, while others break out in a cold sweat. But all of them appreciate the fact that they'll be prepared for what to expect in terms of their emotional reactions when they actually compete.

Not coincidentally, the pros who can see themselves suc-ceeding in their A.I.M. imagery exercises usually perform better and finish higher on the leaderboard—even if they don't end up actually winning—than those who can't see themselves winning.

You don't have to be a teaching pro or a trained sports psy-chologist to understand why. It's common sense that if you A.I.M. for disappointment and failure, you'll almost surely suffer disappointment and failure. A.I.M. for success, and you're more likely to enjoy success.

All right then—let's A.I.M. for success as we use imagery to refine and improve your full swing, short game, and putting in the chapters ahead.

CHAPTER ②

the full swing

THE SWING
IS A SYMPHONY

Perhaps the single most important A.I.M. image to keep in your mind's eye as we learn about the fundamentals of the golf swing is that it's just that—a swing. Like any other type of swing, including swinging on a porch or playground swing, the golf swing is a dynamic movement, a fluid, continuous motion from beginning to end.

In this chapter, I'll focus in detail on the key parts of an ideal full swing: posture, grip, alignment, the waggle, the takeaway, the wrist cock, the top of the backswing, the downswing, the impact zone, and the finish.

But in a golf swing, the whole is greater than the sum of its parts. All the components must work together to create one precisely and smoothly coordinated action. Every great golf swing is like a symphony: It has an overall rhythm, tempo, and pacing that ties the separate notes together into a mellifluous composition.

Far too often, high-handicap golfers and even top tour players get confused and frustrated by an overload of mechanical swing thoughts. Their golf swings degenerate into a disjointed jumble of separate parts lacking unity, coordination, timing, and that all-important sense of "feel." In golf, mechanics and technique are vital—but they should and must play second fiddle to the dynamism and flow of the swing itself.

As we cover the full swing, I'll refer to the concept of sequencing, a term that describes the order in which the parts should move. In teaching proper sequencing, I like to use the acronym C.A.S.H., for clubhead, arms, shoulders, and hips. The A.I.M. images presented in this chapter will help you make your C.A.S.H. flow.

Along the way, you'll get the best results, and improve fastest, if you can incorporate A.I.M. images into each and every one of your practice swings as well as into the swings you make with a golf ball in front of you. That's how you develop feel. Good players pay close attention to the process of making their practice swings thoughtful, meaningful, and real. A practice swing is a reminder of what you've been working on and a dress rehearsal of what you're going to do when you actually play the game.

As you strive to improve your full swing, A.I.M. for the feel of swinging on a swing and for the dynamic dress rehearsals you see in the practice swings of top tour pros such as Davis Love III.

"Mechanics and technique are vital—but they should and must play second fiddle to the dynamism and flow of the swing itself."

❶ Hit It into the Expanse

Imagine the free-flowing motion your swing would have if all you were trying to do was hit the ball into an open area such as a lake or canyon, with no trees or fairway and therefore no need to consider direction or distance. Bring this sense of freedom and fluidity into your practice swings—and carry it over into the dynamic movements of your full swing.

POSTURE

I always focus on posture first because good posture allows for a good swing to take place. Unfortunately, the reverse is also true. Poor posture can be the beginning of all sorts of problems that can have a domino effect throughout the rest of your swing.

Posture sets up your grip, stance, and alignment. It allows you to use the length and lie angle of the club to establish proper ball position and the appropriate distance to stand away from the ball. Simply put, posture is a required component, a platform to not only allow but also create a good swing.

Just as the golf swing has a dynamic look and feel, proper posture has an elegant look and an athletic feel. A.I.M. for the athletic elegance of Tiger Woods's posture.

① Tip off the Barstool

A good way to get into your posture is to imagine yourself tipping forward off a barstool. Just be sure to tip off the front edge of the stool rather than off the middle of the seat cushion so that you create the proper spine angle at address.

❶ Balance on Air Disks

When you take your address, find your center by imagining yourself balancing on a pair of air disks so that you engage and enlarge the quadriceps muscles in your thighs. In fact, I recommend purchasing a pair of real air disks and using them to improve your balance and posture.

ⓘ Make Footprints in the Sand

To further promote balance and stability in your stance when you take your address posture, imagine that you are "standing heavy"— heavy enough to make footprints in the sand. This will lower your center of gravity and steady your stance.

Ⓐ See Your Shoelaces

If your knees are properly flexed when you assume your posture, you should be able to see a bit of the laces of your shoes when you look down. If you also see your socks, your knees are too stiff. If you can't see any shoelaces, your knees are too flexed.

Ⓜ Lift Your Left Pocket

When your spine is properly tilted to the side in your address posture, you should be able to clearly see that the left pocket of your pants is higher than the right pocket when you look in a mirror head-on. This will help ensure that your weight is properly distributed and that your head is behind the ball at address and at impact. I'm holding a 5 iron in this photograph. With a driver, I see slightly more of my left pocket and left side. With a pitching wedge, I see slightly less.

Ⓜ Line Up on the Shaft

Once you've taken your address posture, check your balance by hanging a 5 iron from the middle of your right shoulder, and look in a mirror from a down-the-target-line angle. The shaft should line up with the outside edge of your right knee and the ball of your right foot. If the shaft hangs in front of your right foot, you've got too much weight on your toes. If the shaft hangs behind your right knee, you're sitting too far back on your heels.

THE GRIP

Your grip is only as good as the posture that frames it. When you set up to the ball with an unbalanced, misaligned posture, your grip will most likely suffer. By the same token, a poor grip itself can cause all sorts of problems, while a good grip will complement your setup and allow you to get the most out of your swing and your game.

The most important aspect of the grip is how you place your left hand on the club. Start by holding the club in front of you with your right hand just below the grip. Make sure the leading edge of the clubface is squarely aligned. Then bring your left hand to the grip and place the butt end of the grip just below the base of your left little finger, going up through the first joint of your forefinger. Properly placing the left hand will allow you to achieve the maximum hinging motion with maximum control. The right hand simply slides into the place that the left hand provides for it. By placing the lifeline of your right palm on top of your left thumb, you will be able to wed your hands together.

Your grip is what links you to the golf club, so there should be no "loose connections," no gaps between your hands or your fingers. A.I.M. for the classic "no gaps" look of Arnold Palmer's grip.

Ⓜ One Hand at a Time

How to Grip the Club

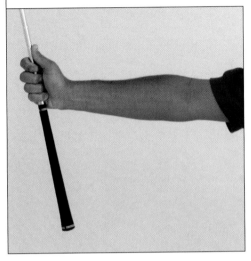

1. Hold a club perpendicular to the ground and at arm's length in front of you, with your right hand on the shaft, just beyond the lower end of the grip.

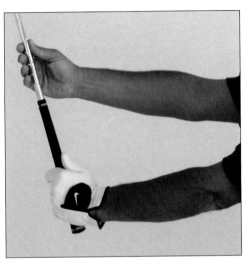

2. Place your left hand on the grip so that your left thumb is pointing up the right side of the grip. Allow the grip to cross the first joint of your forefinger and run gradually into your palm. Your left wrist should be fully cocked.

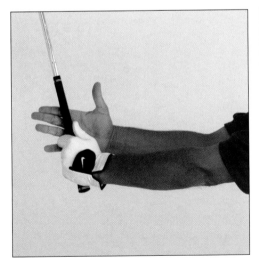

3. Place the lifeline of your right palm over your left thumb.

4. Close your right hand around your left hand. My preference is the overlap grip, where the little finger of the right hand is behind the knuckle of the left forefinger. Now your grip is secure.

Ⓜ Airtight, No Daylight

When your hands are properly wedded in your grip, you should see no gaps between your fingers. In effect, your grip should be airtight and impenetrable by daylight. The club will be secure in your fingers, but your wrists will still be able to hinge effectively.

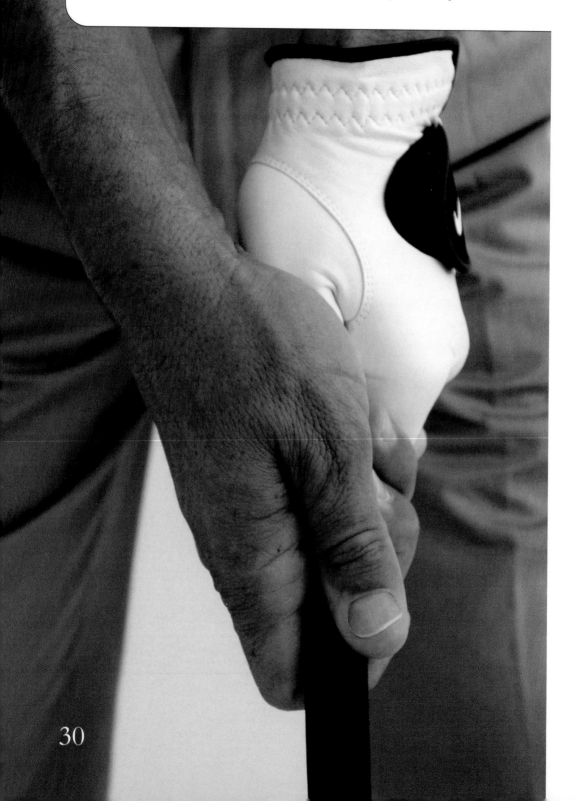

Ⓜ A Little Bit of Butt

When you look in a mirror from the down-the-target-line angle, you should see a little bit of the butt of the club—roughly $1/8$ inch—extending from your left hand. That indicates you're gripping the club correctly in the fingers of your left hand. If you see more of the club's butt, you're probably gripping the club too much in the palm of your left hand rather than in your fingers, or simply too far down the shaft.

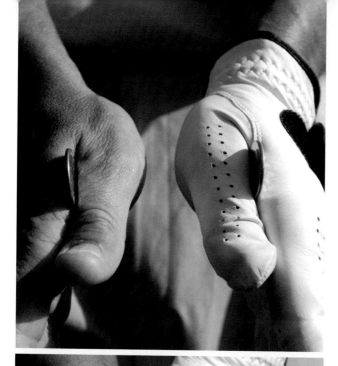

Squeeze the Toothpaste

When you grip the club, imagine you are trying to gently squeeze toothpaste out of a jumbo-size tube. You can grip with as much firm pressure as you like so long as you don't tense up. You'll know you're gripping too hard if you feel your facial muscles tense up.

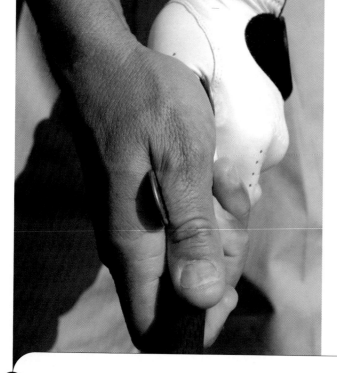

Keep the Coins between Your Thumbs and Forefingers

When you hold the club, imagine you are holding a coin between the thumb and the side of each hand. This image, a favorite of former PGA Championship winner Steve Elkington, will help you achieve a classic "no gaps" grip.

Knuckles, Nails, Cup

When you hold the club in front of you and look at your grip, you'll know it's correct if you can see two to three knuckles on your left hand, the nails of the middle and index fingers of your right hand, and a bit of cup in the back of your left wrist. If you can see any more or any less, your grip is either too weak or too strong.

33

Ⓐ See the Crooks of Your Elbows

You'll know that your posture and arm position at address is correct if you can see slight crooks in your elbows as you look down. If you can't see any elbow crooks, your arms are too stiff. This can create too much tension, rounding your chest and pulling you out of the ideal posture.

ALIGNMENT

Alignment is the term for correctly setting your body angles in relation to the club and your target. While maintaining a dynamic posture, you want to make sure that you line up your upper body and lower body. The extremities of your alignment are your arms and feet, so pay close attention to them as well.

Ideally, you should align yourself with the same basic procedure every time. Set the clubface toward the target first, and then align yourself perpendicular to the club. By following this sequence in your alignment routine, you'll find it much easier to set your body parallel to the target line.

To hit consistently accurate shots, you need to have a consistent and accurate alignment routine. A.I.M. for the precision you see in Jack Nicklaus's alignment routine.

1 Make Your Clubface Reflect Your Target

As the first step in your setup, imagine that the face of your club is a mirror, and set it behind the ball so that it "reflects" the image of your target. Now set your body perpendicular to the leading edge of the clubface as you take your stance and posture.

① Tilt the Ladder

As you establish your alignment, imagine that you're holding a ladder tilted parallel to your thighs and your target line.

37

Ⓜ The Thighs Have It

Many golfers try to check their alignment by laying a club on the ground, across their toes, but that can be misleading because it doesn't accurately account for the position of the rest of your body. I believe you get a much better check of your alignment by laying a golf club across your thighs and then looking in a mirror from a down-the-target-line angle. The shaft should be parallel to your target line. If it's pointing left of your target line, you're aimed left, and if it's pointing to the right, you're aimed right. You can see how "the thighs have it" with the two simple alignment crosschecks on the facing page.

Lay a club across your shoulders....

Then hold a club in front of your eyes. If your thighs are already parallel to your target line, the shaft lines across your shoulders and in front of your eyes should be parallel to the target line as well.

Ⓜ Let Your Logo Be Your Guide

The logo on the left breast of your golf shirt allows you to establish proper ball position in reference to your spine rather than in reference to your feet. For a driver, the ball should be left of the logo, in line with your left armpit.

Ⓐ Brim Line Your Target Line

You can use the brim of your cap to check your alignment on the full swing (and on your putting stroke). Simply roll your eyes upward without altering your posture or stance, and visualize a line connecting the left and right tips of your cap's brim. That line should parallel your target line.

For a 5 iron, the ball should be directly in front of the logo's midpoint.

For a 9 iron, the ball should be just off the right edge of the logo.

THE WAGGLE

Almost all good players use a waggle as part of their pre-shot routine. A waggle is simply movement of the clubhead with very little movement of the grip end of the club. This ritual will eliminate any excess tension in your arms and allow you to transmit the feel of the shot you are about to hit. For instance, a slow, soft waggle serves as a rehearsal for a slow, soft swing. While waggling, exhale to release any tightness from your body.

Your waggle is a signal to yourself that you're ready to start playing the game. A.I.M. to mimic Mark O'Meara's waggle.

❶ Shake the Fly off the Foam Tube

As you make your waggle, imagine yourself trying to shake a fly off the tip of a foam tube. Your body should waggle in the opposite direction of your hands and arms, and you should feel downward pressure on your feet for better balance and power. In a good waggle, the grip end of the club moves only a little, but the clubhead moves a lot.

43

❶ Blow Out a Cloud of Breath

To release tension in your waggle, imagine yourself blowing out a cloud of breath on a cold or foggy day.

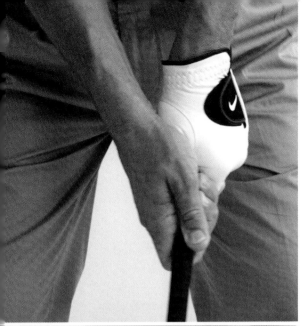

ⓂKeep Your Hands inside the V

When you waggle the club, be sure to move only your hands, keeping them inside the V formed by your inner thighs. Some players also promote their feel for the rhythm of their swings by tapping their toes gently on the ground or regripping the club.

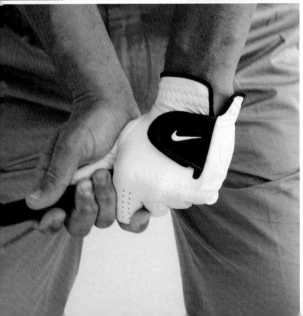

ⒶSoft Focus Your Eyes

As you waggle, soft focus your eyes on the general area around the ball rather than fixating on the ball and staring at it. Your soft focus will reduce pre-shot tension.

THE TAKEAWAY

Your takeaway sets the tone for your entire swing, initiating the tempo, the path on which the clubhead moves, and the plane in which the club shaft travels. It's all about fluid motion and correct sequencing.

Here's where we return to the acronym C.A.S.H. that I mentioned in the introduction to this chapter. In a proper takeaway, the sequencing should be clubhead–arms–shoulders–hips, a prescription that will keep your swing on path and on plane by ensuring an orderly chain of physical actions. If I had to pick a dominant movement, I would advocate that the left side initiates the takeaway and, at the same time, the right side resists.

The keys to a good takeaway are being smooth and graceful. A.I.M. for the smoothness and grace of Steve Elkington's takeaway.

❶ Swing the Bucket but Avoid a Spill

When you start your takeaway, imagine that you're gradually swinging a bucket back without spilling any water. To do this, your hands, arms, and shoulders must move in sequence. If you swing the bucket with only your arms, or if you rotate your forearms too much, you'll splash water on the ground. In the wrist cock phase of your backswing, you will want to spill the water, but not early in your takeaway.

47

❶ Open the Fan

Imagine your takeaway as similar to opening a large fan. With the top edge of the fan standing in for the club shaft and the bottom edge of the fan representing an extension of your left arm, you can picture how the club moves a greater distance than your arm does.

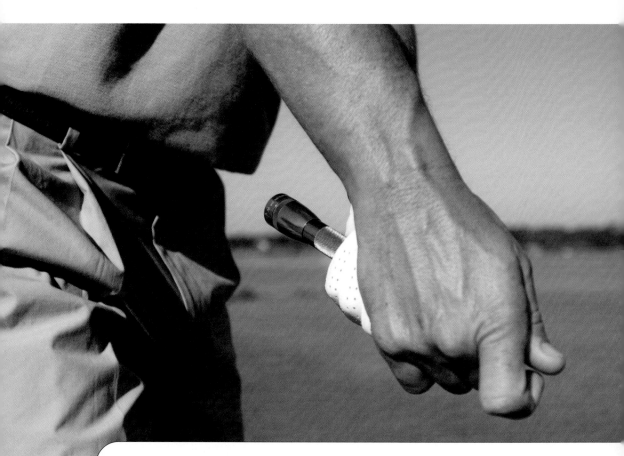

Light Your Tummy

Imagine a penlight attached to the butt end of your grip. It should shine on your abdomen throughout your takeaway. If you jerk the club away or lift it too soon, the light will shine away from your tummy.

Ⓐ Keep the Clubhead outside Your Hands

When you look down during your takeaway, you should see that the clubhead is still outside your hands but slightly inside your target line.

Ⓜ Narrow the Gap between the Tee and Your Right Hip

Insert a tee in the hole in the butt of your grip, and swing through your take-away. If you look in a mirror from a down-the-target-line angle, you should see a narrowing of the initial gap between the tee and your right hip, indicating that you're keeping your arms close to your torso and the clubhead outside your hands.

THE WRIST COCK

The wrist cock is the phase of the swing when you should focus on getting the club on plane. By that I mean getting the shaft balanced so that it closely resembles its original plane angle at address.

By the time your left arm is halfway through the backswing and parallel to the ground, your wrist hinge should be virtually completed and the grip end of the club should be pointed down at a spot somewhere between your toes and the target line. In order to achieve this, pay attention to hinging both wrists, with your focus on the butt end of the club pointing more down than out.

Ideally, your wrists should cock in the same way and at the same time on every swing with a particular club. A.I.M. for the sequenced repeatability of Nick Faldo's wrist cock.

🅘 Keep Away from the Cactus

Imagine there's a cactus plant attached to the right side of your back during the wrist cock phase of your backswing. It's vital to maintain some separation between your right elbow and your right side to keep your swing radius wide. If your right elbow moves too close to your torso, you'll stick yourself with the cactus needles.

I Drain the Pipe Gradually

In the wrist cock phase of your backswing, imagine you're gradually draining water from a shaftlike pipe that matches the proper plane angle of your swing. The water should flow out somewhere between your feet and the ball. If you swing back too flat, the water will barely drip out, and if you swing back too steeply, the water will pour out too fast.

Ⓜ Bisect Your Right Biceps

You can check that your club is on the proper plane during the wrist cock phase of your backswing by looking in a mirror from a down-the-target-line angle. You should see your hands in front of your chest and the club shaft bisecting your right biceps.

Look at the Leading Edge

In the wrist cock phase of your backswing, it often helps to stop and check the clubface. Ideally, the leading edge should be at the same angle as the shaft.

THE TOP OF THE BACKSWING

The position you achieve at the top of the backswing is often spoken of as if it is a still position. Of course, it is not a static position, because as you achieve the top of your backswing, your downswing is underway. However, knowing what your ideal backswing should look and feel like is most beneficial.

Complete the move to the top of your backswing feeling as if your club, arms, and shoulders arrive there together. To see that you are on the right track as far as the line of your swing is concerned, there are certain checkpoints you can look for, such as the clubface position, your swing radius, your coil, and your pivot.

A.I.M. for the extended but relaxed position Ernie Els achieves at the top of his backswing.

Ⓘ Point the Hose

It's time to revisit the image we used as an introductory exercise in chapter 1. Imagine yourself holding a garden hose and attempting to squirt water at your target from over your right shoulder as you reach the top of your backswing. This puts you in an ideal position, with plenty of coil and a nice wide arc.

1 Throw the Football

Imagine that you're coiling to throw a football as you reach the top of your backswing. The majority of your weight should be over your right side, with your body fully wound to store power.

Ⓜ Maintain the Triangle between Your Arms

If at the top of your backswing you look in a mirror from a down-the-target-line angle, you should see a nicely balanced and comfortably wide triangle formed by your right arm and left forearm. Also, look for the angle of the leading edge of the clubface to match the plane of your left forearm, and for a minimal gap between your knees.

❶ Point a Pencil

Imagine that you have a pencil in your mouth (or, as a drill, actually put one in your mouth). Point the pencil at the ball at address, and then move it so that it points toward your right shoe as you reach the top of your backswing. To do this, you must allow your head to rotate to the right, enhancing your weight shift and coil.

Ⓐ Cover Your Right Shoe

If you're fully turned and coiled onto your right side at the top of your backswing, you'll see that your left shoulder will be covering your right shoe as you look down from your stance. This indicates that you have shifted toward the right side at the top of your swing.

Ⓜ Gradually Let Go

You can cross-check your top-of-the-back-swing position by grad-ually letting go of the club: It should fall across your right shoulder.

THE DOWNSWING

The downswing is the phase of the swing when you start to deliver the clubhead to the ball. The key word here is "start." The downswing is a move that must be made gradually and without any sense of hurry so that all the component parts of your swing continue to work together in unison for optimum power and accuracy.

There is no magic move from the top. But just like the start of the backswing, there is a sequence of movements closely linked together, from the left knee and shoulder unwinding to the arms changing direction and moving down, allowing the club to fall into plane.

This change of direction also possesses a lazy, un-hurried look that camouflages the stored power. A.I.M. for the unhurried, gradual pace of Sam Snead's classic downswing move.

I Drop the Pig and Catch Its Tail

You can emulate one of Sam Snead's classic moves by pretending that you are squeezing a pig between your legs at the top of your backswing. As you start your downswing, your goal is to drop the pig by moving your left knee. To do this, you'll have to make Snead's "power squat" with your legs. Then try to catch its tail between your knees at impact with the ball by releasing your right side through the impact zone.

67

❶ Keep the Chair Propped off the Ground

Imagine that you're propping a chair off the ground as you make your downswing. That will require maintaining the correct spine angle down through your buttocks and feeling downward pressure with your legs.

 **Look for the Lag**

If you stop halfway through your down-swing and look in a mirror, you should see the shaft of the club underneath your right shoulder and a sharp angle formed by your arms and the shaft. That's lag. The sharper the angle, the more lag—and the more potential hitting power—you've stored.

Ⓐ Keep Your Right Wrist Up

Another good way to check on how much lag you've created is to stop your down-swing when your right elbow is in front of your right hip. Look down at your right wrist: It should be bent upward or "held" as if you are holding the club back.

THE IMPACT ZONE

The impact zone begins just past your right knee and extends just beyond your left knee. The moment of impact with the ball is merely one point along this continuum. If the sequencings in the earlier parts of your swing have been properly set in motion, it will feel as if the club is traveling through the impact zone virtually on its own.

What happens right before and right after the actual moment of impact really tells how well you release, or swing through with, your hands, body, and club. A.I.M. for the level head and body in Ben Hogan's move through the impact zone.

❶ Paint a Line

To encourage a good and level extension of your right side and enhance both the power and accuracy of your shots, imagine that you're painting a line with your right hand and arm as you swing the club through the impact zone.

❶ Chop a Tree

As you swing the club through the impact zone, imagine that you're chopping the trunk of a tree with an ax, allowing the centrifugal force of the ax to force you into the ideal hitting position. You should feel as if your body is getting ready to absorb the hit, with your arms fully extended, your head still, and your feet pushing into the ground. This image is particularly useful when you are using your driver.

Ⓐ Watch It

It's almost impossible to see the clubhead strike the ball if you're swinging at full speed, but you should try nonetheless. Just making the effort will help keep your head level and your spine angle stable through the impact zone. After impact on an iron shot, you can certainly see the divot you've made.

Ⓜ Please Release Me

You can tell whether you've properly released the club by checking in a mirror when the clubhead is at the far end of the impact zone. Both arms should be fully extended and your spine should be at about the same angle as at address. Have a look at the position of the clubface as well. It will tell you volumes about the quality of your release. Ideally, it is just slightly turned to the left.

THE FINISH

The finish of your golf swing is the result of all the sequencings that you previously put in motion, starting with your waggle and your takeaway. It is also a good barometer of what happened during your swing.

Ironically, I sometimes find that my students get more out of their finish—and more out of their golf swing— if they reverse the old cause-effect axiom. Focus solely on making a full and balanced finish and you may be surprised to find that you somehow manage to make a full and balanced golf swing. Who knows why? It may simply boil down to the fact that knowing where you're trying to go makes it easier for you to get there, with less effort and less conscious thought along the way.

You should have the feeling that you've fully expended all your energy and motion by the time you finish your swing. A.I.M. for the fully released look of Sergio Garcia's finish.

① Wrap a Scarf

As you make your finish, imagine that you're wrapping a scarf over your left shoulder, encouraging a full release of your right hand and arm and a complete follow-through.

Ⓜ Point the Clubhead Where the Ball Used to Be

Look in a mirror to see where your clubhead is pointing at the finish of your swing. If you've made a full finish, it should be pointing at the spot where the ball was before you struck it.

❶ Sword Fight

After you complete your follow-through, imagine that your club is a sword and that you're recoiling it back down in front of your eyes, bisecting the pin. This will mean you've fully released the club and maintained good posture throughout your swing.

79

Ⓐ See the Ball Flying to the Target

If you've made a good golf swing with a fully released finish, your head and eyes should be slightly tilted on an angle that matches the plane angle of your swing, and you should be seeing the ball flying toward your target.

CHAPTER ③

putting
and the
short game

THE NAME OF THE GAME

When golf is the name of the game, the object, as we all know, is to get the ball into the hole with the fewest possible strokes. Playing the game requires both power and finesse in every shot you make. Generally speaking, the full swing provides the power you need to move the ball from tee to green. Putting and the short game provide the finesse you need on and around the green.

In this chapter, we'll cover all the main facets of the short game, including chipping, pitching, and bunker play. We'll begin with putting because it's the stroke you use to get the ball into the cup on every hole—unless you're lucky enough to hole out from off the green.

In putting, finesse is far more important than power. By my definition, finesse is a combination of accuracy, touch, and feel. There's no question that accuracy, touch, and feel are needed in driving the ball. But if you miss a fairway with your drive, you don't automatically lose a shot. You can still make a par or a birdie from the rough or from a fairway bunker. There is no forgiveness in putting. You either make the putt and record a final score on the hole or miss the putt and lose at least one shot on the hole.

Paradoxically, a putting stroke is similar to and diametrically different from a full swing. Both require rhythm, tempo, and timing. As in a full swing, all the components of a putting stroke must work together to create a continuous flowing motion. But in putting, the role of the body, which helps produce power in the full swing, must be deliberately limited for the sake of finesse.

From a mechanical point of view, I believe the key to good putting is to keep your body quiet and your head still throughout your stroke. The steadier your head and body, the easier it is to make a smooth, consistent putting stroke that rolls the ball toward the hole on the proper line with the proper speed.

I also believe that attitude far outweighs mechanics when your ball is on the green. Confidence is everything in every aspect of putting, from reading greens and lining up your putts to making solid contact with the ball. Confidence is supremely important under pressure, whether you're putting to win a $2 bet from your weekend foursome or putting to win the U.S. Open. Lack of confidence breeds indecision, inconsistency, and missed putts.

As you work to improve your putting, A.I.M. to focus on accuracy, touch, and feel, and make the confident rap of the putting stroke Tom Watson used to win eight major championships.

> "As in a full swing, all the components of a putting stroke must work together to create a continuous flowing motion."

Ⓘ Tap the Thumbtack into the Ball

As you prepare to make your putting stroke, imagine there's a thumbtack protruding from the back of your ball. Your goal is to tap the thumbtack firmly into the ball. A favorite image of Ray Floyd, this will encourage proper acceleration and solid contact with the ball and boost your confidence by providing a focus for your putting stroke.

POSTURE AND SETUP

Putting is the most personal stroke in golf. Every golfer, pro or amateur, seems to have their own unique way of going about it and their own favorite tool for doing the job. Regardless of what type of putter and putting style you favor, you must be able to putt the ball where you want it to go.

As in the full swing, posture and alignment are crucial in putting. You should feel relaxed and comfortable when you stand over a putt; stiffness and tension destroy finesse. You should also be sure to address the ball with your shoulders and forearms aligned parallel to your target line so that you can roll the ball on line.

When you set up to stroke a putt, A.I.M. to emulate Brad Faxon's relaxed posture and on-target alignment.

❶ Create a Sidewalk Box with Your Stance

Imagine you're standing on a sidewalk box as you take your putting stance, and simply square your feet and shoulders with the box. This will help you establish correct alignment and accurate aim on every putt.

I Drop a Marble on the Ball

You can determine the proper ball position for putting by imagining that you're dropping a marble from your left eye as you take your stance. This marble should land directly on top of the ball you intend to putt.

87

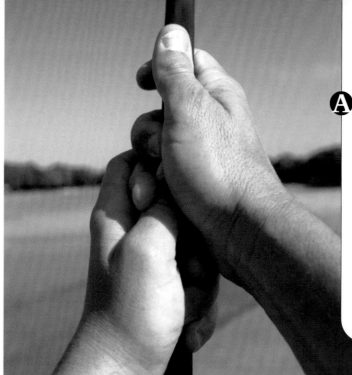

Ⓐ See Gaps in Your Grip

When you look at your putting grip, you should see the palms of your hands opposing each other, and you should see gaps between the thumb and forefinger of each hand. Where the "no gaps" grip used on a full swing helps your wrists cock, a putting grip should help reduce wrist hinge to keep the putter on path.

Ⓜ Be on the Balls of Your Feet

Keep your weight forward on the balls of your feet when you take your putting stance. This will help you keep the putter on line throughout your stroke. Checkpoint: If you can lift your heels without losing your balance, your weight is properly on the balls of your feet.

Ⓜ Keep Your Eyes and Thighs inside the Line

When you look in a mirror from a down-the-target-line angle, you should see that your eyes are inside the target line or directly on top of it, but never outside the target line. I also use another reference point: I make sure that the angle formed by my thighs matches the shaft plane angle of my putter.

Ⓐ Align with the Logo Line

For accurate alignment, line up the logo line printed on the ball with your target line and the aim line on your putter blade.

STROKE PATH, FACE ANGLE, AND IMPACT POINT

Most putting strokes can be divided into two types: "line" path strokes that move straight back and straight through, and "arc" path strokes that curve around the body in a semicircle. I recommend the arc stroke for reasons I'll explain in the following section.

But I also want to emphasize that path has relatively little influence on the outcome of a putt. The angle of your putter face (square, open, or closed) at impact with the ball is far more influential. So is the point of impact on the putter face (center, toe, or heel).

Bobby Locke hooked his putts on an arc path, and the young Jack Nicklaus shoved his putts on a line path, but both men enjoyed great success. A.I.M. to emulate them by contacting the ball in the center of your putter blade with the face square to your target line.

Ⓜ The Plane Truth about Putting Strokes

Look in a mirror while holding a putter and a driver side by side. The putter is the most up-right club in your bag, but like the driver, it still has some shaft plane angle—which means that its design is suited to stroking the ball on an arc path. On short putts, you may feel as if the putter is moving straight back and straight through on a line path. But the longer the putt and the longer your stroke, the more your path will arc because of the putter's shaft plane angle.

I Stick a Popsicle Stick through Your Watchband

As you make your putting stroke, imagine you've stuck a Popsicle stick through the watchband on your left wrist. This will ensure that you keep your left wrist firm instead of flipping it. Although it's against the Rules of Golf to use teaching aids on the course, you can use a real Popsicle stick to do this as a drill on the practice putting green before you tee off.

Ⓐ Right Thumb the Right Line

If you were to grip the club with your right hand only, you would ideally see your right thumb pointing down the path of your stroke as you look down from your putting stance on your follow–through. This indicates that you kept your putter face square throughout your putting stroke.

Ⓐ Hold Your Finish

Determine to hold your finish after every putting stroke. This will help you hold the putter face on line. It will also give you instant feedback on the quality of your contact and the position of your putter face.

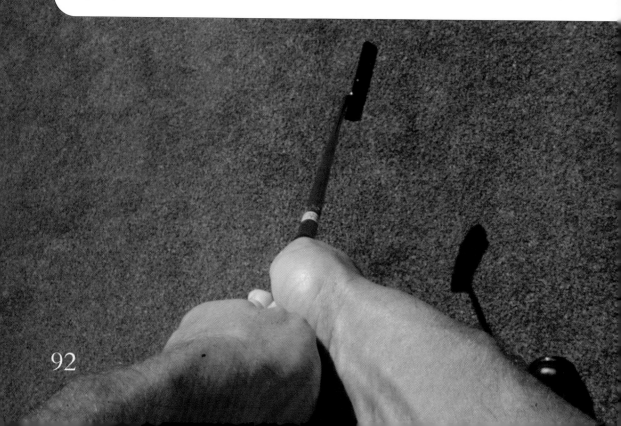

Target Line, Speed, and Green Reading

Let's suppose we're having a playing lesson on a par-4 hole. Thanks to paying relaxed attention to the fundamentals of the full swing, you've hit your ball onto the first green in 2 shots, and it's come to rest about 20 feet from the cup.

Now it's time to sink that birdie putt.

You and I start examining the texture and slope of the green. As it happens, the cup is located on a gentle rise on the right side of the putting surface. You have an uphill putt that appears to break to the right.

"How far outside the left edge should I aim my putt?" you ask as I walk over to tend the pin for you.

I answer your question with a bemused grin and another question.

"Well, how hard are you going to hit it?"

Every time you prepare to stroke a putt, the two main considerations to keep in mind are the speed at which you want to roll the ball and the target line on which you want to roll it. Many of the best putters on the pro tour insist that speed is more important than line, especially on long putts, where distance is usually harder to judge than the overall direction of the break. As a rule, most amateurs pay too much attention to line and not enough attention to speed.

In reading greens, speed is also more important than break. The speed at which your ball will roll is influenced by how hard or soft you hit the putt, the length of the grass and the direction of its grain, the overall slope of the terrain, and the strength and direction of the wind. Most of the above factors can also influence the direction of the break, but speed can override break. The faster the ball rolls, the less it will break. The slower the ball rolls, the more it will break.

When you read greens and pick the target lines of your putts, A.I.M. to follow the speed-sensitive approach of a world-class putter like Ben Crenshaw.

Ⓐ Tend to Speed Before You A.I.M. Your Putts

The amount of break you should play depends on the speed at which you intend to roll your ball.

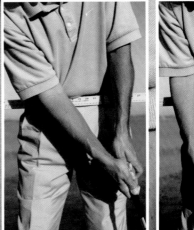

I Follow the Ruler

Imagine there's a ruler across your waistline, and focus on moving the putter equal distances back and through on every putt—for example, 3 inches and 3 inches on a short putt, 6 inches and 6 inches on a longer putt. Be aware that the putter head will probably move farther in each direction than the grip end. Move the putter back and through on a level plane. This will give you another tool for gauging the correct distance.

I See Balls and Cups

When deciding how much break to play on a makeable-length putt, imagine the distance you intend to aim left or right of the hole in terms of a golf ball's diameter, which is 1.68 inches. Since you will have a golf ball on the green (or in your hand, if you've marked your ball), you've got a ready-made visual aid that's easier to use than trying to estimate the break in inches.

When deciding how much break to play on a longer or big breaking putt, imagine the distance you intend to aim left or right of the hole in terms of a cup's diameter, which is 4.25 inches. Since you've got a cup right there on the green, cups are easier to visualize than feet or yards.

AROUND THE GREEN

Like putting, the short game demands more finesse than power. It calls for accuracy, touch, and feel. And as in putting, developing accuracy, touch, and feel in your short game requires practice. You can't practice your short game too much, and amateurs generally practice it far too little. Tour pros devote at least half of their practice time to their short games.

The basic tools of your short game are your pitching wedge, your sand wedge, and your lob wedge. Today's wedges come in a vast array of design characteristics, lofts, lie angles, and bounces. As a rule, tour pros carry at least three wedges with relatively even loft gaps—for example, a 48-degree pitching wedge, a 52-degree gap wedge, and a 58-degree sand/lob wedge.

If you carry only two wedges, be aware that the loft gap between a 48-degree pitching wedge and a 56-degree sand wedge is the equivalent of two clubs, or roughly the same as the loft gap between pitching wedge and 8 iron.

At the same time, be aware that virtually every club in your bag is a potential short game tool, including your fairway woods. The short game is all about adaptability and creativity. As you hone your short game, A.I.M. for the adaptability and creativity of players like Chi Chi Rodriguez and Lee Trevino.

CHIPPING

The difference between a chip shot and a pitch shot is the ratio of ground time to air time. In a chip shot, the ball travels a greater distance on the ground than in the air. In a pitch shot, the ball travels a greater distance in the air than on the ground.

The key factors determining shot selection are the type of lie you have and the location of the hole relative to the fringe of the green, bunkers and hazards, and undulations on the putting surface. When deciding between a chip and a pitch, your preference should usually be maximum ground time, minimum air time. Chips are easier to control than pitches because they reduce variables such as wind and the bounce of the ball on impact with the ground.

Chipping requires the same green-reading skills as putting, with a bit more strategic planning. Before you chip, try to determine the optimum finishing point for the ball. Depending on the speed and break of the green, some chips can be offensive in nature, while others must be defensive. Whatever chipping situation you encounter, A.I.M. for the imaginativeness of Phil Mickelson's chipping.

Ⓜ Right Shoulder Forward

As a chip shot has a low trajectory, you should position the ball inside your right toe and opposite your right shoulder. Your right shoulder should be farther forward than for a full swing, and you should keep most of your weight on your left side. Keep your stance slightly open and grip down on the club. This will encourage crisp contact with the ball.

Ⓐ See the Shaft Bisecting Your Left Shoe

As you look down from your chipping stance, you should see the shaft of your club bisecting your left shoe. This is a good way to check that your stance is correct and your hands are ahead of the ball.

99

🅘 The Rule of Chipping

When you're chipping, imagine a ruler across your waistline, just as you did in one of your putting images. The grip end of the club should move equal distances back and through. But in contrast to a putting stroke, in which you release your hands and the putterblade after impact, when you chip you should make sure to keep your hands well ahead of the clubhead at all times.

ⓘ Stick a Popsicle Stick through Your Watchband

Imagine you've stuck a Popsicle stick through the watchband on your left wrist when you're chipping. As with the Popsicle stick in our putting image, this will help you keep your left wrist firm and make solid contact. And here again, you can also convert this image into an actual drill on the practice chipping area.

M The Putt-Chip

In pressure situations, try the putt-chip. Grip an 8 iron with your putting grip, tip the clubhead up on the toe, play the ball back in your stance, and make a relatively short, straight line swing similar to a short putting stroke. This will deaden the blow and make the ball come out lower. You'll get the hang of the putt-chip quickly by using a mirror to check that you've properly toed the clubhead (rather than soled it) when you address the ball.

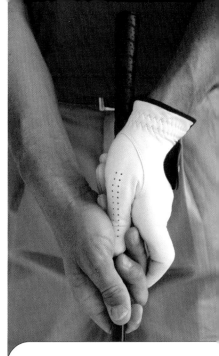

Ⓜ A Fairway to Chip

One of the fairest, most forgiving, and most versatile ways to chip is with a fairway wood, especially if your ball is on the fringe of the green. Use your putting grip and grip down on the club so that your hands are almost on the shaft, then tip the clubhead away from you so that the heel is off the ground. You can tell if you've properly tipped the clubhead by looking in a mirror from a down-the-target-line angle: The grip of your fairway wood should be aligned with your left forearm. From a head-on angle, you'll see that half of the club grip is visible above your hands, in the same plane as (though not strictly parallel to) your left forearm. With a little practice, you'll get the feel of chipping with a club that's lighter than a wedge or a short iron.

PITCHING

In pitching, there is a premium on trajectory control because the ball spends more time in the air than on the ground. Be aware that pitching is much less forgiving than chipping. You've usually got a relatively small area within which to land the ball for optimum results, and the texture of the putting surface (soft or firm) will have a major influence on how the ball bounces when it lands and where it finally comes to rest.

It's also important to adjust your spine tilt to create a fairly steep angle of attack so that you can get the ball into the air more easily. As the following photos illustrate, it helps to keep your stance open and most of your weight on your left side. You can calibrate the distance of a pitch shot with your hand position on the club grip: The more you grip down, the shorter the ball will go.

Since a pitch shot requires a longer swing than a chip shot, there is an added premium on efficiency of motion to promote accuracy and consistency. A.I.M. for the efficient motion of Tom Kite's pitching.

Ⓘ Light a Match

When pitching, imagine that the ground below the ball is the strike board of a matchbox and your club is a giant match. Try to "light the match" with your pitching motion so that you make a crisp stroke.

I Slalom on Snow Skis

When you address a pitch shot, imagine you're slaloming on snow skis. Point the toes of both feet past the ball, and keep most of your weight on your left side.

❶ Drop a Marble on the Ball

You can determine the correct ball position for a pitch shot by imagining that you're dropping a marble from your right eye. The marble should land directly on top of the ball you intend to pitch.

106

I Softball Your Pitch

When you make a pitch shot, imagine you're tossing a softball underhanded in a slow-pitch softball game. Just as the form is similar, so is the rhythm—slow, smooth, and unhurried. You can do this as a drill with a real softball to develop a feel for short-distance shots.

ⓜ Keep the Clubhead in Front of Your Hands

On a short pitch shot, you should see the clubhead in front of your hands if you look in a mirror from a down-the-target-line angle. This indicates that you've taken the club back on the correct track.

Ⓐ Keep the Clubhead outside Your Hands

When you finish a pitch shot, look at the position of the clubhead on your follow-through—if you've kept your wrists firm and properly limited your forearm rotation, the clubhead should always be outside your hands on your follow-through.

ⓘ Three Ways to Throw In the Towel

You can use an imaginary towel in three ways to improve your pitching.

1. Wrap the towel under your armpits to feel the correct link between your arms and body.

2. Lay the towel a few inches behind the ball to promote a steep angle of attack.

3. Land balls on the towel to improve your feel for distance and accuracy.

GREENSIDE BUNKER SHOTS

In a greenside bunker shot, the object is not to hit the ball but to hit the sand around and beneath the ball. To do that, you need to align your body to the left, aim the clubface to the right, and cut across the ball with an early release. I advise most club players to limit practicing their bunker shots so as not to ingrain habits that might adversely affect their full swings.

When preparing to execute a bunker shot, you need to adjust your stance, setup, and ball position appropriately as illustrated in the following photos. Play the ball forward in a greenside bunker shot so the club will bottom out in the sand in front of the ball. Widen your stance and maintain plenty of flex in your knees to lower your center of gravity. Dig your feet into the sand; the shorter the bunker shot, the deeper you should dig in. Hold the club with a stronger left-hand grip and a weaker right-hand grip so you can keep the clubface open. Lower your hands and keep them behind the ball to add loft.

You'll start to love bunker play like the pros do if you A.I.M. to emulate Seve Ballesteros's low hands setup.

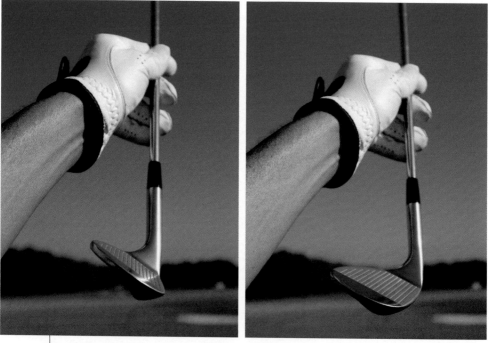

Diggers and Skimmers

Every sand wedge has two principal design features: (1) a leading edge, which is the lower metal ridge on the front of the clubface, sometimes called a digger, and (2) a flange, which is the mass of metal forming the sole and the trailing edge, sometimes called a skimmer. Bounce is the amount of slope between the leading edge and the trailing edge, measured in degrees (6 degrees is low; 12 degrees is high). You'll immediately improve your bunker play by knowing which design feature is appropriate to the basic types of lies you're likely to encounter. Use the digger to dig the sand out from under the ball on buried lies. Use the skimmer to skim the sand out from under the ball on standard explosion shots.

Standard Explosion Shots

(A) Cover Your Shoelaces with Your Knees

If you've set up to a greenside bunker shot with the right amount of knee flex, you should see your knees covering your shoelaces as you look down from your stance.

❶ Balance the Wine Glass on the Clubface

When making a standard explosion shot from a greenside bunker, imagine that you're trying to balance a wine glass on the face of your sand wedge at address and through impact. This will encourage you to keep the clubface open through impact and promote the necessary underhanded release.

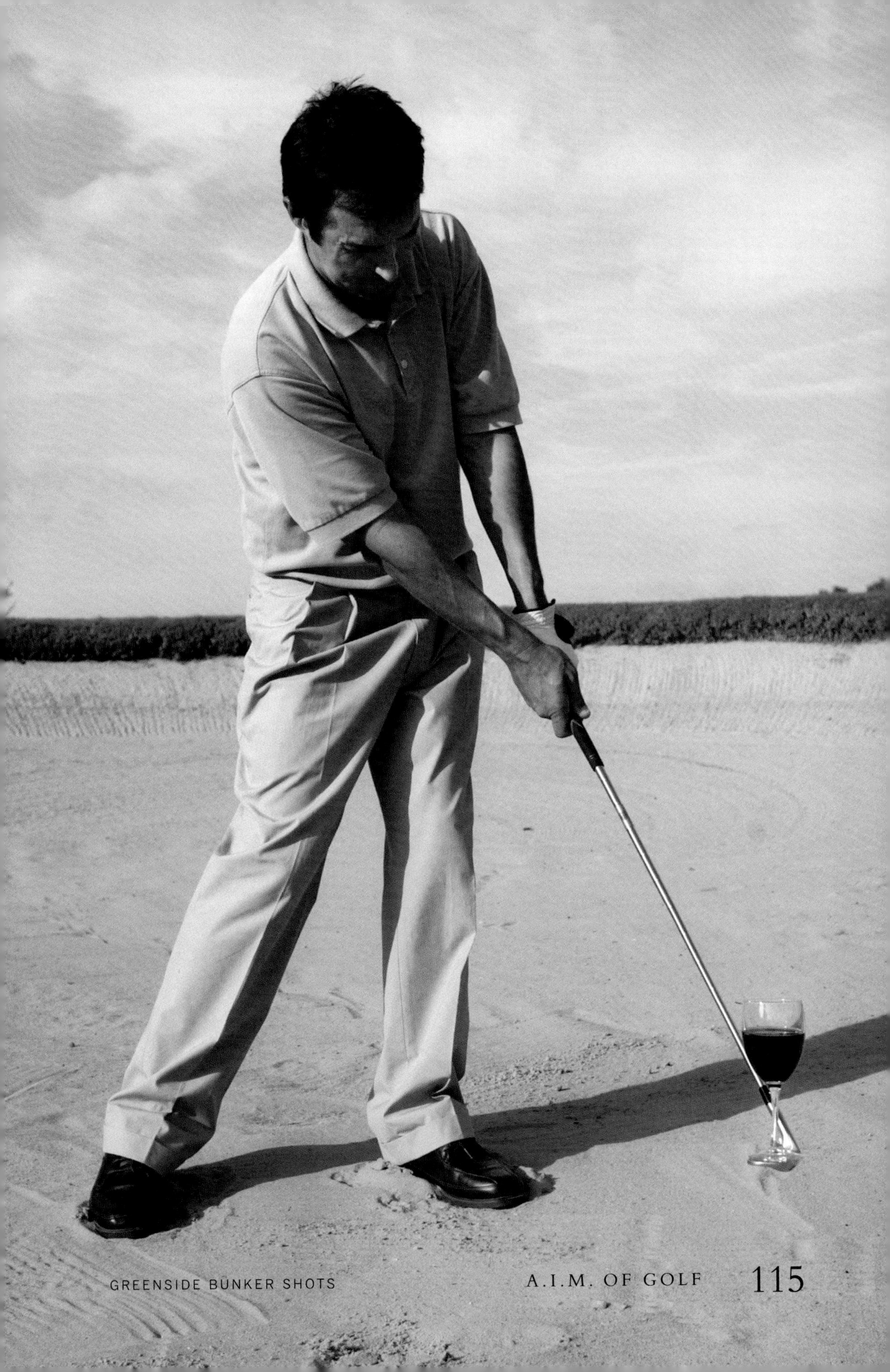

Ⓜ Hands behind the Ball

Looking in a mirror head-on, you should see your hands behind the ball and your thumbs pointing forward as you take your address for an explosion shot from a deep greenside bunker. This helps keep the face open, making the ball pop out higher.

❶ Toss the Pyramid of Sand over Your Right Shoulder

Imagine there's a pyramid of sand on the face of your sand wedge at address. Then imagine you must toss the pyramid of sand over your right shoulder. This will encourage you to keep the clubface rotating open throughout your backswing.

Downslope Lies

Ⓐ Swing down the Slope

When faced with a downslope lie in a bunker, you should open the clubface and focus your eyes on a point just beyond the ball, then make a long backswing and a short follow-through. Caution: The ball will come out low and fly to the right, so adjust your aim accordingly.

Upslope Lies

Ⓐ It's Hip to Be Square

When facing an upslope lie in a bunker, you should see a square clubface and a square stance as you look down. Two notes of caution: First, the slope will increase loft to your shot and decrease its overall distance; second, be ready to hit and step back so you don't get sand in your eyes.

⚠ Land a Fish

When facing an upslope lie in a bunker, imagine that you're trying to land a fish with your follow-through. This will help you keep your body behind the ball and the club swinging upward after impact.

120

Buried Lies

I Swing inside the Phone Booth

When facing a buried lie in a bunker, you want to create a steep angle of attack and limit your follow-through. Here you can apply the time-tested image of swinging inside a phone booth without hitting the booth's walls.

drills and specialty shots

A.I.M. Your Work and Play

In this chapter, we'll learn a variety of drills that will help you hone your basic skills and correct any lingering problems with your full swing, putting, and short game. Given the fact that a high percentage of average golfers are slicers, I've included a special section called Slicers' Corner.

Just as important, we'll practice specialty shots such as intentional draws and fades. You'll learn images and drills for hitting out of fairway bunkers. I'll also share a few of my favorite "Top Secrets" for extra power off the tee and sharper scoring on and around the green.

You'll get more out of A.I.M. imagery and your practice sessions if you make your practice fun—as much of a game as golf itself. Pretend that the shots you hit in your practice drills are to win the U.S. Open or your club championship. Create realistic practice situations. Find a tree, and practice hitting fades and draws around it until you've mastered both options. Don't just stand out on the range walloping drives. Emulate the tour pros by spending at least half your time on putting and your short game; that's by far the best and quickest way to lower your scores on the golf course.

It's no accident that the world's best player is also the world's best and most creative practicer, always eager to spend hour upon hour honing every facet of his game. As you practice your drills and specialty shots, A.I.M. to enjoy the creativity of Tiger Woods's practice sessions.

> "Make your practice fun—as much of a game as golf itself."

FULL-SWING PRACTICE DRILLS AND FIXES

❶ Match the Pro

You can improve the rhythm and tempo of your swing by "stealing" the rhythm and tempo of a pro or other good player you run into on the practice range. Stand behind the pro and cross your arms in front of your chest. Turn your body back as the pro swings back. Then turn your body through as the pro swings through. You'll probably be surprised at how slowly you have to turn in each direction to match the pro. Bring that same rhythm and tempo to your own swing.

I Stand with Your Heels on a Two-by-Four

To promote correct posture and spine angle at address, imagine standing with your heels on a two-by-four—or find a real two-by-four and actually use it as a practice aid.

❶ Heel the Two-by-Four

Imagine a two-by-four pointing parallel to your target line, and heel the board (don't toe it) to ensure proper alignment. Here again, you can actually use a real two-by-four as a practice aid.

129

Check Your Alignment with Two-Tone Shoes

To check that you're lining up parallel to your target line, practice on the range in two-tone shoes.

1. Square stance: The toes and saddles of your shoes match up, indicating correct alignment.

2. Closed stance: The toe of your right shoe is even with the saddle of your left shoe, indicating that your feet are too far to the right.

3. Open stance: The toe of your left shoe is even with the saddle of your right shoe, indicating that your feet are too far to the left.

❶ Roll the Peach

Good rhythm starts with a good takeaway. To improve the smoothness of your takeaway, imagine there's a peach positioned directly behind your ball at address, and gently push the peach away without bruising it.

Lose Track of Time

If on your takeaway you have a tendency to be quick and snatch the club away from the ball, imagine there's a watch on your left wrist, and simply limit your forearm rotation so you can't tell the time on the face of the watch as you start to swing back the club.

Ⓐ Keep the Toe Up

In a good takeaway, you should see the toe of the club pointing up as you look down from your stance, indicating that you're moving the club back on the correct path.

❶ Toss the Spuds

To improve your backswing, imagine you're tossing a sack of potatoes to someone standing directly to your right. This will help you feel the shift of momentum to your right side during your backswing that sets up a powerful coil and helps keep the club on plane. You may actually want to practice with a real sack of potatoes or even a medicine ball.

Ⓜ Hitchhiker Arms, Back and Through

To maintain the ideal club path and plane, you should try to keep both thumbs pointing up like a hitchhiker signaling for a ride as the club is halfway through your backswing and as it passes waist high on your follow-through.

Ⓜ It's a Stretch

A great drill for increasing the torque on your backswing is to hold a 5 iron with the butt of the grip in your left hand and the clubhead in your right hand, and then swing the club back and hold your stretch. This is also a great warmup drill.

137

Ⓜ Halfway Back, See Your Right Shoulder

The wrist cock phase of your backswing is a good point to stop and look in a mirror to check your sequencing. You should be able to see your right shoulder in the mirror as you look head-on, indicating you've made just the right amount of shoulder turn.

(M) Cross-Handed Pivot Practice

You can practice coiling by crossing your left hand over your right hand and turning back to the top of your backswing. If you look in a mirror head-on, you should see your left shoulder has moved to the right of your left hip.

I Carpenter's Level Hips

As you make your backswing, imagine there's a carpenter's level across your hips, and try to keep the bubble in the center. This will help you get the feel for maintaining a level hip turn.

Ⓜ Turnabout for Fair Play

Look backward into a mirror at the top of your backswing. Your belt line should be relatively level, indicating you've made a compact and level body turn.

ⓘ Spill the Waiter's Tray

To enhance your feel for the proper hand and arm position as you reach the top of your backswing, imagine that you're spilling a waiter's tray. Contrary to popular belief, in the correct position, your right arm is not at an angle suitable for supporting a heavy object such as a tray. Ideally, your right forearm should be at the same angle as your spine. The ideal clubface angle is represented by the angle of the tray.

❶ Skip the Stone

To improve your swing motion through the impact zone, imagine that you're skipping a stone. To do this, your right elbow must lead your right wrist in a sidearm sweeping motion. You'll quickly gain a feel for the extension and straightening of the right arm through impact.

SPECIALTY SHOTS

I Turn the Steering Wheel for a Draw or Fade

If you want to hit a draw, imagine that you're turning a steering wheel to the left during your follow-through.

If you want to hit a fade, imagine that you're turning a steering wheel to the right in your follow-through motion.

144

I Straddle the Footrest to Hit It High

To hit a high-trajectory shot, position the ball forward and imagine that you're straddling a footrest, widening your stance and lowering your center of gravity.

❶ Skim the Ironing Board to Hit It Low

If you want to hit a low-trajectory shot, position the ball back slightly and imagine there's an ironing board positioned above it, perpendicular to your target line. Then scrape the board through impact.

FAIRWAY BUNKER SHOTS

 **Chin Up, Feet Flat**

When you address the ball in a fairway bunker, you should keep your chin up and grip down on the club about an inch so that you make contact with the ball before the club clips the surface of the sand. You should also strive to keep your feet flat from start to finish so that you maintain a more level body as you release the club.

Ⓐ See the Ball, Not Your Feet

When assuming your stance in a fairway bunker, you should remain relatively erect so that you see only the ball and not your feet as you look down, ensuring that you'll strike the ball first, not the sand.

❶ Swing on Ice Skates

When playing a shot from a fairway bunker, imagine that you're swinging the club while standing on ice skates, keeping your thighs solid to prevent excessive body movement. The object here is the opposite of a standard greenside bunker shot: You want to hit the ball first, not the sand. Position the ball in the middle of your stance or slightly forward (but never back of middle), use one extra club, grip down, and keep your wrists firm. Swing level to sweep the ball out of the sand. The ball's flight will be slightly lower than from a greenside bunker, so make sure to choose a club with enough loft to clear the lip in front of you.

Slicers' Corner

① Left Foot on the Phone Book

If you've been slicing your drives, imagine that you've got your left foot on a phone book when you set up to the ball. This will help you keep the majority of your weight on your right side at address and keep you behind the ball through the impact zone.

Ⓐ See Three Knuckles for a Draw

A stronger grip will encourage a draw. See three knuckles on your left hand as you look at your grip.

Ⓐ Shadow off the Ball

On a sunny day, you can check your swing by looking at your shadow. Check your posture and club plane at the top of your backswing. Check to see whether you have made a complete turn to your right side and maintained distance between your right arm and your torso.

❶ Swing the Flagstick

Imagine you're swinging a flagstick instead of a golf club. Slicers often swing too steeply, and the sheer length of the flagstick will force you to flatten out your swing. Here again, you can convert image to reality by actually swinging a flagstick.

I Crack the Whip for a Big Hit

Perk up your power by imagining that you're cracking a whip when you swing your driver. Remember that you've got to wait for your downswing to develop to get the right whip crack.

157

TOP SECRETS

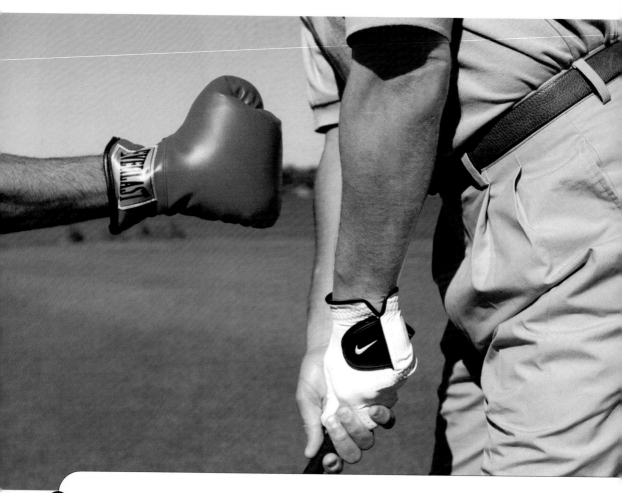

❶ Fist in Your Stomach

For more power off the tee, imagine someone is punching you in the stomach at the climax of your waggle, forcing you to breath out through your mouth and tuck in your abdominal muscles. Tension in your hands and arms kills power, and this image will help you relocate your pre-shot tension to your core muscles, where it can actually enhance balance and power.

Ⓜ Separate Your Shoulder and Chin

Looking in a mirror head-on, you should see your shoulder separate from your chin during the initial phase of your downswing. Practice this move to maintain the width of your swing arc, creating extra power and distance.

① Swing the Light Saber for Longer Drives

Let the Force be with you for longer drives by playing Luke Skywalker with a real or imaginary light saber. It should remain retracted to maintain lag halfway into your downswing.

As your wrists uncock, the blade should shoot out at impact.

Ⓐ Grip off the Tip for More Power

You can add power to your drive by gripping off the tip of the club, promoting a sharper wrist angle and more lag through the impact zone. Caution: You may sacrifice a bit of accuracy and control.

If you're after more power and distance, it's vital to focus on rhythm and tempo so that you improve your ability to make solid contact with the ball in the center of the clubface on every swing. Try this one-two timing drill.

Move your left shoulder under your chin on the way back, and count "One." Then at impact, count "Two."

PUTTING AND SHORT GAME PRACTICE DRILLS

❶ Putt to Your Partner's Bird Feet

When you putt, imagine your playing companion is standing bird-footed behind the hole. This will encourage you to stroke the ball firmly to the cup. As the old saying goes, never up, never in. This image translates into a great drill—get someone to actually stand behind the cup on the practice green.

 Putt It on the Nose

To groove your stroke path and improve the centeredness of your contact, practice putting with the nose of your putter instead of the face. Try this from about a 4-foot range.

I **Putt to the Garbage Can Lid**

To improve your feel for pace and direction on long lag putts, imagine there's a garbage can lid over the hole.

I Putt off the Hood of a VW Bug on Superfast Greens

When you encounter superfast or severe downhill greens, imagine you're putting from atop a Volkswagen Beetle. How softly do you have to stroke the ball to gently slide it down the hood?

ⓘ Pitch into an Upside-Down Umbrella

You can improve your pitch shots by imagining that your target is an upside-down umbrella. As you perfect your pitching motion, aim for specific panels on the umbrella. My aunt Marley used to use a real umbrella for a practice drill.

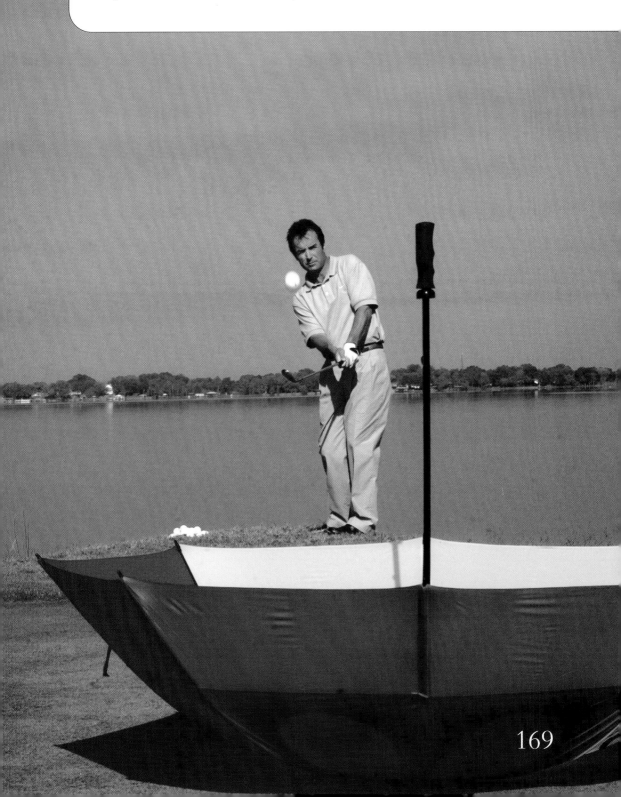

Ⓐ Knock the Ball off the Tee

A great drill for improving trajectory and distance control on your pitch shots is to line up a dozen or more balls at varying distances and try to knock a ball off a tee peg stuck on the surface of the green. You should see the clubhead outside your hands on your follow-through.

❶ Chip down the Staircase

When faced with a chip shot to a superfast or downhill green, imagine that you're chipping your ball down a staircase with the A.I.M. of making it stop on one of the steps.

❶ Skim a Buck out of the Sand

In a bunker, imagine there's a dollar bill lying directly below your ball. Try to enter and exit the sand on the ends of the bill, and you'll skim your ball and the buck right out.

172

Final Thoughts

The more familiar you become with identifying a good swing, the easier it will be for you to produce a good swing—hence my references, throughout the book, to the tour players whom I think you should imitate in terms of key swing components, from posture and grip through impact and finish.

As you work on your game, there will be clues to your progress. But you must know where to look for these clues. One obvious place is the scores you shoot out on the golf course. Ultimately, we all want to shoot lower scores more consistently. That said, your scores can be misleading if taken out of context. No golf course is exactly the same from one day to the next. Weather, course conditions, pin placements, and demands on your course management skills can and will affect your score in every round you play.

I'd prefer that you look to your ball striking, rather than your scores, for the leading barometer of your progress in improving your swing. Are you making solid contact with the ball more often? When you don't make solid contact, are your mishits generally better and a bit less off-line than they used to be? Can you control the distance of your shots better than in the past? Do you keep the ball in play more consistently than before? These are the kinds of questions you should ask yourself during or after a round.

Your practice and warm-up sessions are also fairly reliable measures of your progress. I believe that the first few swings you make when you step out on the practice range give great insight into the true state of your swing mechanics. I also believe that you'll make faster and more lasting progress if you take the time to make several deliberate practice swings before you take a swing at a ball. Find a point of focus that you want to work on each day, and make that the theme of your practice and warm-up sessions.

Never start your practice or warm-up sessions by swinging full-bore with a driver—you won't stretch your muscles properly and you may wind up injuring yourself. Start with a short iron and work your way up, hitting no more than 10 balls with every other club (for example, wedge, 9 iron, 7 iron, 5 iron, 3 iron, 3 wood, driver). Here again, to get an accurate gauge of your progress, pay as much attention to the quality and number of your mishits as you do to the quality and number of your solidly struck shots.

Obviously, the acid test is taking your game from the practice range out to the golf course. You'll know you're heading in the right direction when you start to see more power and consistency in your shots, better distance control, a more efficient short game, tidier sand play, fewer putts. As these parts of your game come together, you'll start to put together runs of a few good holes, then several good holes, then entire good rounds. Your ability to keep these runs going more often will soon reflect itself in your scores.

In the following sections, I present photographs of the full swing according to type: actual, imaginary, and mirror images. The best way to utilize these sections is to browse through a selected sequence of images before you practice or play. The photographs will serve as reminders of the various components of the swing, quickly installing themselves in your subconscious and making you more likely to post those sought-after lower scores.

Actualize
YOUR BEST GAME

The old saying "What you see is what you get" is especially applicable to golf. When you're out on the course playing the game, your own eyes are usually the best—and often the only—available monitors of what you're actually doing (unless you have a caddy or playing partner who's also a qualified instructor). Most golf books present photographs taken solely from the perspective of a third party—an "outside" pair of eyes, if you will. This is the first book to offer a comprehensive sequence of images depicting what you should actually see with your own eyes, from the perspective of your own stance, to get the best possible results from each swing.

In order to get maximum benefit from the actual images you yourself see, you need to know what to look for. Golf demands precision. Even the slightest flaw in your grip, alignment, swing path, or clubface position can be the difference between a perfect shot and a frustrating mis-hit. If properly informed and trained, your eyes can give you the kind of precise detail that's crucial to good shot making. When you know what to look for, you won't have to be so reliant on that ineffable, often elusive form of feedback commonly called "feel." You'll be able to trust your eyes—and, more important, your swing.

Let me hasten to add that I'm not advising you to move your eyes around during your swing. When you're out on the course, your eyes should remain focused toward the back of the ball. On the practice range, however, it's a different story. That's when you can and should move your eyes around. On the range, you have the luxury of being able to make stop-action and slow-motion practice swings. You can check various key aspects, particularly your grip, takeaway, and clubface positions. You can compare what you're seeing with what you ought to be seeing from the perspective of your own stance as illustrated by the unique actual images on these pages. With a little repetition guided by these photographs, you'll quickly develop a clear, coherent vision of what an ideal swing should look like through your own eyes.

> **"WHEN YOU KNOW WHAT TO LOOK FOR, YOU WON'T HAVE TO BE SO RELIANT ON THAT INEFFABLE, OFTEN ELUSIVE FORM OF FEEDBACK COMMONLY CALLED 'FEEL.'"**

the full swing

Posture
See Your Shoelaces

The Grip

Knuckles, Nails, Cup

See the Crooks of Your Elbows

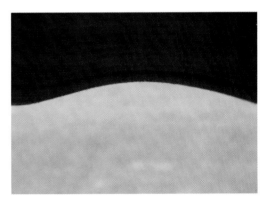

Alignment
Brim Line Your Target Line

The
Waggle
Soft Focus Your Eyes

The Wrist Cock
Look at the Leading Edge

The Takeaway
Keep the Clubhead outside Your Hands

The Top of the
Backswing
Cover Your Right Shoe

The
Downswing
Keep Your Right Wrist Up

The Impact Zone
Watch It

The Finish
See the Ball Flying to the Target

Imagine
YOUR BEST GAME

I consider imaginary images to be "child's play" in the fullest, most creative sense of the term. Where actual and mirror images often tend to break down the golf swing into static component parts or idealistic checkpoints, imaginary images tend to be dynamic, action-oriented, holistic, idiosyncratic, and fanciful. Imaginary cues bring all the parts of the swing into a unified, comprehensive, sequentially fluid "mental movie" that is custom-made by and for each individual golfer. They are the exact opposite of traditional, verbally oriented swing thoughts. These images free your mind (and, by extension, your body and your golf swing) so that instead of laboring over each shot with gritted teeth, you can play the game with a grin—like child's play.

When exploring and using imaginary images, let your so-called inner child have free rein. The imaginary images in this book, most of which incorporate familiar everyday objects, are those that I've found to be exceptionally vivid and enlightening. But you can and should dream up imaginary cues of your own. Try to keep them targeted at one specific aspect of your swing or the shot in question. Unlike with actual or mirror images, you don't need a sequence of imaginary images for each shot. There's no need to envision "swing the bucket" followed by "throw the football" and then "drop the pig," because such images are already dynamic and sequential by nature. So keep them simple, focusing on one at a time, not on a clutter.

At the same time, try to keep them as vividly "realistic" as possible. One of my students, an aspiring tour pro, recently faced a difficult lob shot at a critical stage in a tournament. He told me that he had vividly imagined the ball floating into the air and then falling softly onto a pillow next to the pin. Sure enough, he successfully executed that testy shot.

Finally, believe in your imaginary images as if your life depended on it. If you're trying to improve your balance, for example, you might imagine yourself standing on the edge of the Grand Canyon. I can almost guarantee that you won't swing too hard and lose your footing!

> "WHEN EXPLORING AND USING IMAGINARY IMAGES, LET YOUR SO-CALLED INNER CHILD HAVE FREE REIN."

the full swing

Posture

Tip off the Barstool

Balance on Air Disks

Make Footprints in the Sand

The Grip

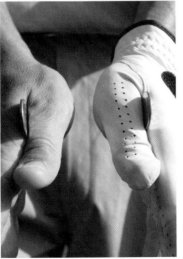
Keep the Coins between Your Thumbs and Forefingers

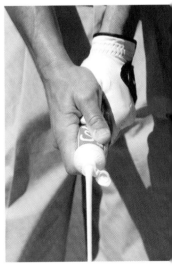
Squeeze the Toothpaste

Alignment

Make Your Clubface Reflect Your Target

Tilt the Ladder

The Waggle

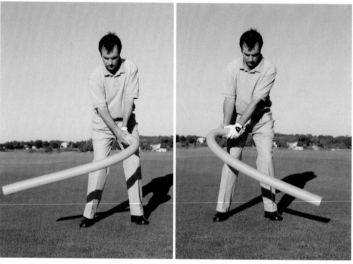

Shake the Fly off the Foam Tube

Blow Out a Cloud
of Breath

The Takeaway

Swing the Bucket
but Avoid a Spill

Open the Fan

Light Your Tummy

The Wrist Cock

Keep Away from the Cactus

Drain the Pipe Gradually

The Top of the Backswing

Point the Hose

Throw the Football

Point a Pencil

The Downswing

Drop the Pig and Catch Its Tail

Keep the Chair Propped
off the Ground

The Impact Zone

Paint a Line

Chop a Tree

The Finish

Wrap a Scarf

Sword Fight

Mirror
IDEAL POSITIONS

I started using indoor mirrors in my family's home to improve my swing when I was a youngster. When I arrived at the David Leadbetter Golf Academy many years later, I found full-length outdoor mirrors set up on the practice range with hitting mats in front of them. Players of every level spent countless hours in front of the mirrors, checking their form; and many of the tour players would also hit balls off the mats in front of the mirrors.

In order for practice to make perfect, we need to strive for perfect practice. I believe a mirror is one of the best aids to perfect practice. After all, "feel" isn't always real: What you feel or sense you're doing with your hands, arms, body, and club isn't necessarily what you're really doing. But a mirror never lies. It always shows you what your grip, alignment, posture, pivot, plane, and positions truly look like. When you witness what you're really doing, you can compare it to what you really want to be doing and gain a better understanding of how your swing should function and appear. What may begin as an unfamiliar position or move quickly becomes familiar, and therefore much easier for you to accept. Perhaps best of all, you can use a mirror to improve your game at home as well as out on the range—you don't even need golf clubs or balls.

Strictly speaking, the mirror images presented in the previous chapters are really straightforward observer's-view photographs similar to those you've seen in other golf books. In the following pages, I'm reversing the film to present you with what are literally mirror images of my swing. I believe you'll gain a whole new perspective from this. For the first time, you won't have to mentally reverse the instructional photos to match your own reflection in a mirror. Instead, you can prop up this book next to a mirror on the practice range or in your home, and simply copy exactly what you see me doing.

> **"I BELIEVE A MIRROR IS ONE OF THE BEST AIDS TO PERFECT PRACTICE."**

The Grip
One Hand at a Time: How to Grip the Club

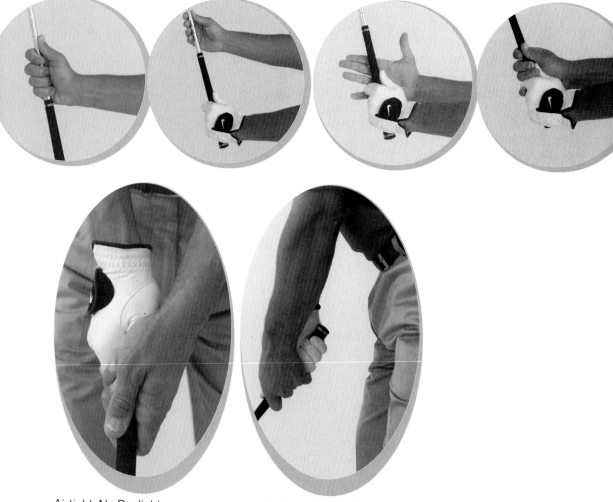

Airtight, No Daylight

A Little Bit of Butt

Posture
Lift Your Left Pocket

Line Up on
the Shaft

The Waggle
Keep Your Hands inside the V

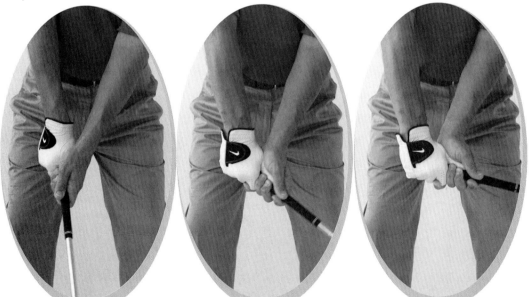

Alignment
The Thighs Have It

Let Your Logo Be
Your Guide

The Takeaway

Narrow the Gap between the Tee
and Your Right Hip

The Wrist Cock

Bisect Your Right Biceps

The Top of the Backswing

Maintain the Triangle
between Your Arms

Gradually
Let Go

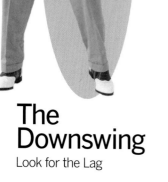

The Downswing

Look for the Lag

The Impact Zone

Please Release Me

The Finish

Point the Clubhead
Where the Ball Used
to Be

Index

Boldface page references indicate photos.